# ADVANCE PRAISE FOR
# STEAM POWER

. . . . . . . . . . . . . . . . . . . . . . . . . . . . . . . .

In *STEAM Power*, Tim helps redefine the role of creativity in the STEAM classroom. He shares his creative insights and practical lessons on how STEAM experiences can impact classroom learning across discipline and department as well as how art educators can evolve their role in giving students the creative mindset and skillset they need to thrive in whatever they do.

Michael Cohen, The Tech Rabbi
Educator, Keynote Speaker. Author of *Educated By Design*

Playful artist and innovative educator Tim Needles brings art from the back seat into the front seat on this STEAM Power journey. From developing a STEAM mindset to implementation considerations to project examples to ways to extend learning, Tim demonstrates how artistic principles can be seamlessly and authentically integrated into STEM curriculum, rather than added as an after-thought. Educators of all disciplines and grade levels will be inspired to begin looking at the world through the eyes of an artist, to make learning fun, creative, and empowering.

Kristina A. Holzweiss
School Library Journal/Scholastic School Librarian of the Year

STEAM POWER indeed! This book offers you an opportunity to participate in an action-packed journey through cross-curricular and multidisciplinary learning. With Tim as your guide, you'll step through the philosophical underpinnings of a truly creative pedagogy and explore meaningful classroom projects full of lasers and oil paint, 3D printers and pencils, computers and cardboard. This text brings ideas to life through engaging illustrations, helpful diagrams, and lessons from real classrooms. There's no talking down to the non-technical here; this guide both inspires and practi-cally supports teachers to engage with the importance of an artful approach to learning powered by STEAM.

Cathy Hunt
Arts Educator, Advocate and Advisor
Founder iPadartroom.com
@art_cathyhunt

Tim Needles provides a beautiful explanation of why the "A" is an integral part of STEAM. People sometimes challenge the addition of the arts but whether you call it STEM or STEAM, creativity is at the center of it all. When designing for an audience it is crucial to consider the aesthetic design as well as functionality. Tim makes it clear that they go hand in hand. Additionally, Tim speaks with the viewpoint of an engineer and an artist and provides practical ways to incorporate the arts in an authentic way, NOT as an afterthought. Thanks, Tim, for your insightful commentary and practical approach!

Steve Isaacs<br>
Teacher, Game Design and Development

For educators looking to get started with STEAM curriculum, the book *STEAM Power* provides the support and resources that will empower educators to provide the best learning experiences for students. In this book, Tim provides a wealth of examples, offers encouragement, and shares many resources that will support educators starting their journey with STEAM projects. Tim shares his own experiences and also includes many other voices through "Teacher Tips," in which educators offer ideas that are adaptable to different content areas and grade levels. Throughout the book, Tim encourages teachers to take some risks with learning and co-learn with students. *STEAM Power* is a very authentic book and provides a thorough overview with many tools and tips for getting started with STEAM curriculum.

Rachelle Dene Poth<br>
Spanish and STEAM Teacher, Consultant,<br>
Author, President of Teacher Education Network of ISTE

With *STEAM Power*, Needles takes us where all schools need to be if we want to succeed in the future—outside of our hedonic adaptation, and into a world of infinite possibilities. *STEAM Power* is an urgent and transformative guide, an essential read for administrators, school board members, educators, parents, and anyone who cares about enhancing the lives of students through art for the world of tomorrow.

Glenn Robbins<br>
Superintendent of Brigantine School District, Brigantine, NJ

Tim's book helped me realize I have the ability to be creative and help students develop a growth mindset in a real-life engaging way! He includes wonderful projects in many different modalities, including building with cardboard, coding, AR/VR creation, designing infographics, video creation, and others. But, more importantly, he provides the reader with the rationale for STEAM, practical processes for implementation, ways to grow as a professional in the STEAM arena, and solid pedagogical methods for utilizing STEAM across the curriculum.

Kathy Schrock<br>
Educational Technologist

*STEAM Power* is my new go-to resource for bringing art into the classroom! With extensive expertise, experience, and passion, Tim guides the reader through a journey of understanding the fundamentals of STEAM and gets teachers right into implementation with his offerings of projects with detailed descriptions, material lists, and step-by-step instructions. All are welcome to join into the experience of infusing art and creativity into learning as Tim shares various perspectives through Administrator's Angle, Professional Perspective, and Teacher Tip sections. *STEAM Power* offers a fresh, innovative take on teaching—supporting all students to be curious and imaginative as they embrace a STEAM mindset!

Jennifer Williams<br>
Co-founder, TeachSDGs and Take Action Global.<br>
Author, *Teach Boldly: Using Edtech for Social Good* (ISTE)

# STEAM POWER

## Infusing Art into Your STEM Curriculum

### Tim Needles

INTERNATIONAL SOCIETY FOR TECHNOLOGY IN EDUCATION

PORTLAND, OREGON • ARLINGTON, VIRGINIA

STEAM® Power: Infusing Art into Your STEM Curriculum
Tim Needles
© 2020 International Society for Technology in Education

Director of Books and Journals: *Colin Murcray*
Acquisitions Editor: *Valerie Witte*
Editor: *Stephanie Argy*
Copy Editor: *Lisa Hein*
Proofreader: *Steffi Drewes*
Indexer: *Kento Ikeda*
Illustrations: *Tim Needles*
Book Design and Production: *Mayfly Design*

The front cover was designed by Eddie Ouellette, incorporating a 3D-printed "STEAM Power," designed and created by author Tim Needles using **Morphi** (morphiapp.com). A video on the making of the "STEAM Power" 3D title is available at youtu.be/Gb0kWUi8jLM or via this QR code:

ISTE Standards Reviewers: April Burton, Susan Elwood, Miguel Guhlin, Billy Krakower, and Vanessa Waxman

Library of Congress Cataloging-in-Publication Data available.

First Edition
ISBN: 978-1-56484-821-5
Ebook version available
Printed in the United States of America
Cover Art: © 2020
Inside Art: © 2020
*Author photo courtesy of Melissa Bellafiore*

# About ISTE

The International Society for Technology in Education (ISTE) is a nonprofit organization that works with the global education community to accelerate the use of technology to solve tough problems and inspire innovation. Our worldwide network believes in the potential technology holds to transform teaching and learning.

ISTE sets a bold vision for education transformation through the ISTE Standards, a framework for students, educators, administrators, coaches and computer science educators to rethink education and create innovative learning environments. ISTE hosts the annual ISTE Conference & Expo, one of the world's most influential edtech events. The organization's professional learning offerings include online courses, professional networks, year-round academies, peer-reviewed journals and other publications. ISTE is also the leading publisher of books focused on technology in education. For more information or to become an ISTE member, visit iste.org. Subscribe to ISTE's YouTube channel and connect with ISTE on Twitter, Facebook and LinkedIn.

## Related ISTE Titles

*Sketchnoting in the Classroom: A Practical Guide to Deepen Student Learning*, Nichole Carter (2019)

*Learning Transported: Augmented, Virtual and Mixed Reality for All Classrooms*, Jaime Donally (2018)

*Make, Learn, Succeed: Building a Culture of Creativity in Your School*, Mark Gura (2016)

To see all books available from ISTE, please visit https://www.iste.org/learn/books.

# About the Author

Tim Needles is an artist, writer, performer, and educator from Port Jefferson, New York. He has been teaching art and media at Smithtown School District in New York for more than twenty years as well as serving as an adjunct college professor. His work has been featured on NPR, in the *New York Times*, the Columbus Museum of Art, the Norman Rockwell Museum, the Alexandria Museum  of Art, the Katonah Museum of Art, the Cape Cod Museum of Art, and The George Washington University Museum. He is the recipient of the ISTE Technology in Action Award, the ISTE Arts and Technology Network Creativity Award, the National Art Education Association AET Outstanding Teaching Award, and the Robert Rauschenberg Power of Art Award at the National Gallery of Art. He has served as a National Geographic Certified Teacher, a PBS Digital Innovator, and an Adobe Education Leader, as well as a TEDx speaker. He is active on social media, guest hosting education chats and sharing his thoughts on arts and education. You can find him on Twitter, Facebook, LinkedIn, and Instagram @timneedles.

## Acknowledgments

Thanks to my editors Stephanie Argy and Valerie Witte for believing in me and helping patiently guide me through my first book. Thanks also to fellow authors David Sedaris, Michele Haiken, Akhil Sharma, and Starr Sackstein for your advice and help in making this book happen.

## Dedication

Dedicated to Melissa, who sat beside me in third grade and is still by my side.

# Contributor Biographies

## Professional Perspective:

**Sophia Georgiou:** Founder and designer of Morphi, a 3D design and printing, augmented reality, virtual reality, and animation app. Sophia is also a designer/entrepreneur in residence at NYIT's Technology-Based Learning Systems, focusing on educational technology, is part of the Fat Cat Fab Lab, one of New York City's top hackerspaces, and Lady Tech Guild, an organization empowering women in technology.

**Lloyd Nelson:** Professional engineer and artist, currently a Federal Project Director at the U.S. Department of Energy for nuclear accelerator upgrade projects working at Brookhaven National Laboratory. He previously worked as a Project Engineer at Grumman Aircraft Systems developing advanced testing technologies and methodologies to support aircraft fabrication.

**Melodie Yashar:** Designer, Researcher, Technologist at SEArch+ / Space Exploration Architecture and NASA Ames Human-Computer Interaction. First place winner in NASA's Phase 1 Centennial Challenge for 3D-Printed Habitat on Mars in collaboration with a team of subject matter experts.

## Teacher Tips:

**Robert Fish:** Educator and Director of Global and Civic Exchange at the Masters School in Dobbs Ferry, New York. Previously, he served as Director of Education and Lecture Programs at New York's Japan Society and Professor of East Asian History at Indiana State University, where he worked extensively with preservice teachers.

**Michele Haiken:** Twenty-year veteran of teaching middle school English and the author of *New Realms for Writing: Inspire Student Expression with Digital Age Formats* (ISTE, 2019).

**Sean Justice:** Assistant Professor of Art Education at Texas State University in San Marcos, Texas. His teaching and research address teacher education in the age of computing and digital networks. As an artist, he has exhibited photographs, videos, and computer animations both nationally and internationally. His book *Learning to Teach in the Digital Age: New Materialities and Maker Paradigms in Schools* was published by Peter Lang in 2016.

**Don Masse:** Elementary art educator at Zamorano Fine Arts Academy, where he regularly introduces students to contemporary artists and practices.

**Kevin McMahon:** Twenty-year digital media educator, ten-year Adobe Education Leader, and the founder of the Design Dojo—a unique, fun approach to design education.

**Ashley Naranjo:** Museum educator at the Smithsonian Center for Learning and Digital Access, with special interests in supporting arts integration across curricula and linking museums to classrooms around the world.

## Administrator's Angle

**Mark Gura:** Author of *Make, Learn, Succeed: Building a Culture of Creativity in Your School* from ISTE. He taught visual art and other subjects in public schools in East Harlem for two decades, developed curricula for the NYC Department of Education, and directed their Office of Instructional Technology. In addition to teaching graduate-level instructional technology leadership courses, he writes for the *New York Daily News*, *Converge*, *EdTech*, *Edutopia*, *THE Journal*, and *EdTech Digest* magazines, as well as for Corwin, Teacher Created Materials, and other publishers.

**Starr Sackstein:** Author, educational consultant, assessment thought leader.

**Barry Saide:** Proud principal of Roosevelt School, in Manville, New Jersey. He has served in leadership capacities as a curriculum supervisor, a director of curriculum and instruction, and a classroom teacher for fifteen years. He is an Association for Supervision and Curriculum Development (ASCD) Influence Leader, an ASCD Emerging Leader, and sits on the state board for New Jersey ASCD and has served as a thought partner on educational policy for the Bill & Melinda Gates Foundation, GreatSchools, the National Council on Teacher Quality, New Jersey Department of Education, and New Jersey Education Association.

# CONTENTS

. . . . . . . . . . . . . . . . . . .

## PART I: STEAM FUNDAMENTALS

. . . . . . . . . . . . . . . . . . . . . . . . . . . . . . . . . . . . . . . . . . . . . . . . . . . . . . . .

## PART II: STEAM PROJECTS AND TECHNOLOGIES

# PART III: NEXT LEVEL STEAM LEARNING

# PART IV: THE STEAM CHALLENGE

# INTRODUCTION

. . . . . . . . . . . . . . . . . . . . . . . . . . . . . . .

*I* remember only a few things from fourth grade: the day I was chosen to work the slide projector (cutting-edge technology at the time), the day kids put glue on my seat, and the day we were asked to create a 3D map of our home, Long Island, New York, with clay, cardboard, and paint. The truth was, from the moment I first entered Mrs. Brush's classroom and saw the example of the 3D project hanging up, it's all I wanted to do in class. I was waiting excitedly for the day I would make one, and when the time came, I took a risk. I chose to lower the hills when they approached rivers because it made more sense to me, but it wasn't in the instructions and my classmates called me out on it. Thankfully, Mrs. Brush made it a teachable moment, shared that it was correct, and approved of my choice. It was an important moment that validated my independent thought as well as my art.

I've been an artist for as long as I can remember. It's always been a part of me, and when I think back on moments, I remember the images and the feelings. These days, I draw in a sketchbook and create with technology daily, and I still love to explore different subjects through art. When I introduce myself to others and they hear I'm an artist, they often ask how much work I sell, how well I draw, or if my work is exhibited in museums or galleries. While I've sold work, draw well, and am proud to have had my art exhibited in numerous museums, I believe none of those criteria make me, or anyone, a true artist. Being an artist is about being curious, examining the world around you, bringing a sense of creativity to what you do and make, and sometimes breaking the rules.

# Overcoming the Fear (and Loathing)

Early on in my educational career, I didn't have much expertise in science, technology, or engineering, but I was always interested in learning more. Math, on the other hand, downright scared me. There are people who love math. I've met them. They just get it, or they find the order and the process appealing. I've also met math-phobic people who dread and loathe math class and often believe they will never be good at math. People in this group benefit tremendously when art is added to the learning process. I know because I was once one of those people.

Let me be clear: I don't want to bash math, because as an art educator for more than twenty years, I know there are also people who fear and loathe art and drawing the way I feared and loathed math. You might be one of those people and if you are, I believe I can help. When I have students who fear art, it's my job to show them that there is more to art than just drawing (though drawing is a skill anyone can learn if they have an open mind and put in time and effort) and, more importantly, that art is an act of personal creative expression that is valuable by itself regardless of the product. You don't need to be good at painting or singing or dancing or acting to enjoy it, learn from it, and benefit. Anyone who has ever tried karaoke or a paint night might know this personally because it is fun and expressive even if it is a train wreck. My advice: own your train wreck! As an artist, I have learned to harness my creativity, and by helping others do the same, I've seen it benefit their lives tremendously. My goal as an educator is always to share my knowledge and to help others cultivate their sense of creativity and curiosity—because once you connect that spark, it fuels the real power of learning.

Many academic subjects address misconceptions, fears, and resistance, but the interdisciplinary nature of STEAM makes it an especially powerful means to address these problems. The first step is identifying the problems and figuring out what they're stemming from. Often, they are irrational or based on false beliefs students may have. The next step is helping students open their minds and change their mindset. Carol Dweck, a psychologist at Stanford University, wrote a book on the topic entitled *Mindset: The New*

*Psychology of Success* that explains the difference between a "fixed mindset," in which people see their talents and abilities as set and static, and a "growth mindset," in which people believe their abilities can be improved through work and study. Dweck shares her research on how we can be held back by the way we think about our abilities and talents, and she notes that "becoming is better than being."

Students often see their failures or weaknesses as permanent, so they don't see the point in trying to improve upon them because it brings forth bad feelings. As a student who didn't naturally excel in math, I understand that reaction. Reflecting on those years, I believe my fear of math was intensified by the fears people around me had about it as well. It wasn't until many years later that I realized that math has a wide variety of aspects, many of which interest me. I learned to not take my early failure in math personally. It didn't define who I was, and once I understood that, I was able to progress and improve.

It is important for educators to understand this behavior of taking failure personally and to address it when it occurs with learners. When students see themselves as bad at something, they often widen the failure and feel bad about themselves in general, as if it's a permanent personality trait. It's hard, if not impossible, to motivate someone to do something that makes them feel bad about themselves, so it often helps to play to the learners' strengths at first to create positive associations. If students have skills or interests elsewhere, find a way to leverage those and connect them with the subject they have difficulty with. It's a process, but the work can be much easier if you remind students that failure is not permanent and if you explain the concept of having a growth mindset.

## How to Use This Book

I offer this book to you as a simple, nonthreatening guide to exploring the world of STEM through art in fun, adaptable, meaningful, and engaging ways that allow for new insights and increased creativity. This book is made up of three parts: The first is dedicated to the fundamentals, giving an overview of elements that will help make the learning successful, safe, and engaging. The second part consists of eighteen of my favorite STEAM projects that incorporate a wide variety of technology, from 3D printing to coding to cardboard and upcycling. The last part is focused on advanced STEAM concepts to expand the learning and grow your program.

## Why Add Art to STEM?

"STEAM" education may seem like a hot trend now, but it's really a new acronym for an ancient educational idea that has been taught since teaching began. The idea of incorporating art into other subjects has been there all along; it's the lens through which we have viewed STEM because it's how this knowledge has been passed down over the ages. If we study the greatest STEM thinkers, we

learn about their work through art, whether it's Marcus Vitruvius Pollio's analyses of architecture, Leonardo da Vinci's sketchbook illustrations, or Albert Einstein's writing on his theories.

In fact, regardless of the subject matter, we often learn through art: images, writing, music, speech, or movement. Art is what we as the human race pass on to the future, and it is how we understand our past. Art has always been there; the issue today is that it's not always easily accessible for teachers or students. This is in part because in our modern educational world with its system of segregated subject matter, art isn't always as valued or supported as STEM in our schools. It becomes an elite language that many don't speak, so it can get sidelined. Art also tends to intimidate people; it only takes one bad art experience to ruin the whole subject for some people and lead to a lifelong avoidance of art.

It may seem unnecessary to justify why art is beneficial to STEM, especially because you are reading this book, but I do encounter a great deal of resistance among some educators. I still regularly find myself in STEAM workshops that don't address art in any way but use the acronym because it's become trendy. When I do see art included in STEAM projects, it's often shoehorned into lessons and not handled with respect, which is frustrating. But recognized experts such as Scratch creator Mitchel Resnick, technologist John Maeda, professor Seymour Papert, and author Sir Ken Robinson have all addressed the importance of creativity in education and the value of art in STEM learning. One of my goals is to offer you valuable tools to infuse art into STEM in meaningful ways that respect each of the component subjects. I've always found that learning new things is rewarding, and it certainly makes teaching much more interesting. As we learn about some of the different ways to infuse art into STEM learning, it's helpful to keep that perspective and have fun learning new art skills.

Infusing art into STEM might be intimidating but as you can see in some of my short videos, introducing it as a fun, creative challenge helps establish a positive mindset and builds excitement.

# PART I

## STEAM Fundamentals

· · · · · · · · · · · · · · · · · · · · · · · · · · · · · · · · · · · · ·

**L**et's begin by discussing the philosophical concepts and tools that are important to developing a successful STEAM learning environment. The way we frame our STEAM learning can make a huge impact on how we learn. In this section, we will discuss how to lay the groundwork to facilitate great STEAM projects, from approaching the work with the appropriate mindset to using the creative process to boost innovation, as well as how to set the tone with the learning environment.

# CHAPTER 1

# The STEAM Mindset

. . . . . . . . . . . . . . . . . . . . . . . . . . . . . . . . . . . . . .

*Harnessing our own creativity offers a new perspective on the world around us. In the world of education, the impact is limitless.*

## Creativity

**I** often hear both students and adults say, "I'm not creative." That fixed mindset isn't just prevalent but also contagious. As someone well-versed in creativity, I always try to challenge that idea and help people develop and strengthen their creative skill set.

If you think about the term "creativity," it's hard to clearly define and can be even more difficult to assess. For our educational purposes, we'll define creativity as bringing a new, unique, and valuable approach to making something or solving a problem.

As an artist, I am very in touch with my ability to be creative because it's a skill I've learned to harness and focus over the years. I often challenge students to produce creative results using the same creativity exercises that have helped me, including making a sculpture with nonart materials, drawing a blind contour (without looking at the paper), or photographing a self-portrait without incorporating their face.

When other educators ask me how they can add more creativity into their teaching, I'll respond with a counterintuitive reply: I suggest they add more limitations. This is one of the easiest ways to inspire creativity, and it can be done in any learning environment. I find that limiting materials and obvious solutions forces my students to find more creative solutions. The same principle of imposing limitations can be used in any of the STEAM disciplines—for example, in projects such as using popsicle sticks to engineer a bridge that can support a heavy weight or estimating the number of windows in a school based on the number in one classroom. This limitation-based approach models challenges that occur in real-world STEAM scenarios, such as how do we build a space station on Mars using only available resources, or what can fit on a spaceship? The idea is simple, but it's an effective way to get learners thinking in new ways. The projects featured in this book all have great potential for bringing out creativity, some through limitations and others through process and design. When you see students making creative choices, point them out to inspire others.

 ## ADMINISTRATOR'S ANGLE
Mark Gura

Any activity in any subject may foster a degree of student creativity. But for activities to nourish and grow student creativity predictably and for all students, teachers have to plan to produce that outcome. Simply assigning an activity that seems "creative" will not likely produce that result—and that includes arts activities. But well-planned music and visual art, for instance, may engage students in doing things that will result in learning things other than creativity: technique, arts appreciation, art history, and response to art, to name a few.

# Art

Creativity is closely related to art, but what is art? This is a necessary question to tackle before proceeding because we don't want to move forward without addressing preconceived ideas that might limit the potential impact of our STEAM learning.

I find many people first associate art with drawing, but it is much more than that. Art comprises a wide variety of disciplines, but at its core are creative expression and communication. As an artist, I love exploring all its facets, from drawing and painting to theater, music, dance, and design. The definition of art has continued to evolve and expand, but whether it's sharing conceptual ideas, documenting history, or skillful decorating by means of sound, images, words, or movement, it's often all about feeling. Art allows for interaction, and like a language, it can communicate and connect ideas.

The writer and philosopher Elbert Hubbard said in his book *Little Journeys to the Homes of Great Teachers*, "Art is not a thing—it is a way." This may give some insight as to why art pairs well with STEM.

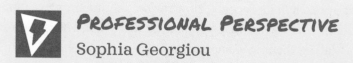

## PROFESSIONAL PERSPECTIVE
Sophia Georgiou

It's hard to imagine having STEM without the *A* in it. I think creative thinking is needed in all of these fields, and they're all equally important and interconnect with each other.

# Failure

We often fear and avoid failure. This is understandable because failing has a host of negative associations and might bring forth bad feelings and shame. But we learn more through failure than we do through success. This is especially important when it comes to STEAM learning because it deals with difficult questions without easy solutions. To innovate and be creative, failure needs to be embraced. To promote creativity, we need to model and share how failing is a part of the process.

We all fail, but not everyone likes to admit their mistakes and even fewer people are open to sharing them. The problem is that avoiding failure means avoiding progress: it keeps us in a safe and familiar area but at a cost. Some people may judge you for your failure and hold it against you, but to move forward sometimes it's necessary to be brave and put your work out there anyway. If we own and accept our failures and share them as a teaching tool to connect with others, we can rise above any negativity. Remember, no one can make you feel bad unless you allow them. Early in my career, I was averse to failure, and it insulated me from growth. I was asking students to take risks and learn from failure and share their process, but I was holding back; later, I made a choice to be more authentic and practice what I preach in its entirety. How can we ask students to embrace and learn from their failures if we don't model it first? We all have fears and we learn from facing them; it's empowering to take them on and learn to persist through failure.

# Curiosity

A core element of the STEAM mindset is being aware of your curiosity and encouraging it in others. Have you ever been going through your day and found yourself wondering about something that you've come across? We all have those moments, and they can be terrific ways to develop new STEAM lessons. It's important to take note of the questions that come up in class, as well as the random curious notions that arise during your day, because they can lead to terrific learning. Questions are a great place to begin a project, especially if you can't find the answers with a simple internet search.

Even seemingly trivial questions can develop into interesting STEAM projects. As an example, I was in the shower shampooing my hair when I had the thought:

*How does shampoo work? I know it's soap, but why are some shampoos more expensive or more effective? What's the science behind it?*

I tried a quick search on the internet and read how detergent molecules bind with the natural oils in our hair. I realized that this might make an interesting question to pose to my students. It's focused on something we all do, generally without thinking too much about it, and it contains an intriguing element of science. If we include the design of a shampoo bottle, the lesson also includes math, art, engineering, and technology. A question such as this can inspire learners to reconsider a part of their daily life, which helps the information to stick.

The framing and implementation of this kind of question will make a big impact on whether it's a success or failure. It's not enough to bring in an interesting question; it's all about the audience and their interests or curiosities. This is why giving students an element of choice is always beneficial for both the educator and the students. I find sharing my curiosity and the process I take for inquiring about the answers is a great way to inspire learners to be curious and develop questions of their own.

## Fun

Fun is one of the best tools that teachers have in their arsenal. Think back to a time that you were learning something and having fun. It may not have been in school, but it's likely that those memories are positive and that you can recall the learning in detail. Don't be afraid of having fun. It sounds like a strange statement to put out there, but I have found a few educators resistant to fun learning out of fear that it might devalue the learning. I've also found some educators fear that they'll be judged if they incorporate fun activities into learning, but have faith that good administrators know when they see impactful, engaging teaching. It's okay to be serious as an educator, but it's also okay to give yourself permission to make learning fun.

Never underestimate the impact fun has on students, especially in a classroom environment. Having fun also frees students up to take creative risks and try something new. STEAM can be a terrific hook to make learning more engaging and memorable. When the learning is fun, the information sticks because it is associated with a positive moment. That makes it more meaningful, so therefore it becomes more ingrained.

We've established that fun is a great teaching tool, but what's the next step? A key is knowing your audience, because what may seem fun and exciting for one group doesn't necessarily translate to another. Fun, like humor, can be subjective, so it's essential to know and feel out the group you're working with. I understand that some educators might be hesitant or inexperienced in this arena, so let's look at the elements that help make a fun project.

**Figure 1.1** Here are a few elements that make for a fun STEAM lesson:

PLAY GAMES
HUMOR ART
MUSIC CHOICE
STORYTELLING
INTERACTIVITY
TECHNOLOGY
MYSTERY MOVING
COLLABORATION

## Design

We are surrounded by design every day—from the clothes we wear to the spaces we occupy—so even if we're not aware of it, we all have extensive experience in the subject. This is why design is such an important and impactful element of art to incorporate into STEAM learning. Design offers a way to bring a creative aspect of art into any lesson or project and add problem-solving, innovation, and hands-on making, which can be educationally transformative. When working with design in STEAM projects, it helps to know and incorporate the basic elements and principles of design to make the work more functional and successful. These include elements such as line, shape, direction, balance, and proportion, which also relate to math and can help students in every type of making. In the Resources section at the end of this book, I've included descriptions of all the elements and principles of design as well as some tools that I use to teach them. In teaching art, I always point out that it is okay to break the rules as you see fit, but it helps to know and comprehend those rules and principles first.

# Design Thinking

My favorite way to demonstrate how design thinking works is to share examples of bad design and examine how they might be designed better. One example uses human movement: Most sidewalks are created in straight geometric grids, so at the intersections where streets cross, the sidewalks meet in perpendicular corners. But often pedestrian foot traffic leaves the sidewalks, creating diagonal shortcuts that cut off the corner. The sidewalk design fails because it doesn't incorporate the user; it might be more successful if the user's movements were studied and incorporated into the design.

One of the benefits of the design-thinking process is that it promotes essential critical thinking and problem-solving skills in students and allows them to incorporate different viewpoints. Using a design-thinking perspective and comparing it with a computational thinking point of view (finding solutions through logic, automation, algorithms, and patterns) can also be an interesting comparison for students and offer them context. Teachers who also use computational thinking in their work may notice how it and design thinking interrelate. The beginning of the design-thinking process is similar to the start of the scientific process: it involves observation and exploration of the situation at hand, which leads to understanding. But the first step in design thinking also includes empathy. Rather than simply looking at the situation, product, or problem, the designer imagines the user's experience, what's involved, and why it matters. It's all about communicating with anyone involved and making sure all the different perspectives and motivations are considered before moving forward. Though often overlooked in real-world designs, this empathy phase may be the most important because it allows us to make the design more meaningful and personal.

Many teachers may comprehend the need for empathy because they have experienced both good and bad design. At times, I've been a part of conversations about making changes in my classroom and been able to share my perspectives. Even if the results weren't exactly what I had envisioned, I felt as though I had a voice in the process and was happy with the design changes. Other times, I've been in situations where classroom decisions were made for me without consultation, and sometimes without even notification, and the design changes made it more difficult for me to teach. As educators, we design lessons and learning for students, so just as we like to contribute our own input and perspectives to situations that affect us, we need to include the voices of our students if we want the best results.

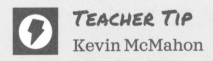

## TEACHER TIP
### Kevin McMahon

• • • • • • • • • • • • • • • • • • • • • • • • • • • • • • • • • • • • • • • • • • • • • • •

Design thinking is more than a methodology for problem-solving. It allows the magical "Aha!" moment of creativity to come more readily and to be more useful.

# Inquiry- and Project-Based Learning

Approaching STEAM with creativity and curiosity engages students and helps ignite authentic learning. While both concepts begin with questions or challenges, inquiry-based learning (IBL) is focused on discovering an answer, while project-based learning (PBL) is about exploring the concept and creating to arrive at an answer. The philosophy is similar in both concepts, but they require different materials and resources. These concepts both allow learners to guide their own learning, which is more active and effective. The role of the educator shifts: the traditional emphasis on facts and memorization is replaced with discussion and self-motivated exploration. This type of learning can help foster curiosity while offering students the chance to take ownership of their own learning, but it requires solid modeling. The educator needs to embrace their own curiosity and authentically share their enthusiasm and love of learning for it to be successful. It requires educators to act more like guides than traditional teachers. Students learn greater self-reliance and independence as they follow their educational path while collaborating, communicating, and learning from other students.

Inquiry-based learning is terrific in building self-direction, and it also offers an opportunity to teach students about data and how to identify quality data, organize it, and summarize it effectively. Project-based learning can be more creative, hands-on, and lead students to a deeper understanding of subjects. These approaches do tend to be less structured and can appear

 **PROFESSIONAL PERSPECTIVE**
Lloyd Nelson

My biggest advice is to keep an open mind. You want to have the ability to keep that learning principle going throughout your life because this opens up opportunities you never knew were going to be around.

like chaos from the outside, so it becomes important for learners to document and share their learning and check in on their progress regularly.

## Standards

When we teach STEAM subjects, it's important to align the learning we do with the various national and state standards in our disciplines, but the ISTE Standards are key in making sure the most important learning and teaching benchmarks are reached. The ISTE Standards are a way to ensure the learning reflects appropriate digital age technology skills and practices and that the learners are provided with fair, safe, and meaningful instruction.

ISTE has five sets of standards—for students, educators, education leaders, coaches, and computer science educators—but in this book, we will focus on alignment with the Student Standards and Educator Standards, both of which can be found online at iste.org/standards. I find that most great lessons naturally align with the ISTE Standards, but it's helpful to refer to the ISTE Standards to confirm that all the essential elements are being covered.

The STEAM projects featured in this book have been created with the ISTE Standards in mind; to make it clear how each project addresses the ISTE Standards, there is an ISTE Standards Project Mapping Guide in the back of the book. You can use this to help you select projects, or you can use it for inspiration as you design your own lessons using the ISTE Standards.

# CHAPTER 2

## STEAM Implementation

· · · · · · · · · · · · · · · · · · · · · · · · · · · · · · · · · · · · · · · · · ·

ow that we've covered the concepts that should be in place before you take on STEAM projects, let's look at some effective strategies and tools.

## A Focus on Materials

Materials themselves can inspire the learning process. Although we can start a STEAM project by considering ideas through writing, sketching, or problem-solving analytics, materials can also serve as the starting point. For that reason, it's helpful to have a well-stocked materials library with a large range of inviting materials, including varied colors and textures that can stimulate visual and tactile learners. Working with nontraditional materials can also be interesting because it allows for scientific comparison.

Experimenting with different materials has led to innovations in STEAM. In 3D printing, technology has expanded from plastic filament to materials such as concrete, chocolate, ice, and even skin. Although classrooms may not be able to work with materials like those yet, we can experiment with different materials, especially when solving problems that relate to real-world issues. An architectural project, for example, could allow learners to examine a variety of materials and how they respond to environmental factors like hurricanes and earthquakes.

Educators can introduce nontraditional materials in a variety of ways, depending on their available resources and the age and skill level of their learners. As learners progress, the approach can become more complex by combining materials, researching emerging materials, and working on innovative solutions to solve problems. I'm currently collaborating with another artist and a science teacher on a project to teach students and the community about where the water that flows into our local storm drains goes. Much of it flows directly into a nearby river; to illustrate that, we considered designing art with text adjacent to the drains on the sidewalks, then I built on that by suggesting we experiment with using hydrochromic paint, which is translucent until it encounters water. When rain falls, a previously invisible part of the design becomes visible. This shift in our choice of material makes the art more interactive, connects it directly with the science, and enables it to make more of an impact.

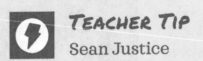

## TEACHER TIP
### Sean Justice

. . . . . . . . . . . . . . . . . . . . . . . . . . . . . . . . . . . . . . . . . . . . . . . . . . . .

In my teaching and artwork, I let materials lead the way to innovation. This remains constant whether I'm working with paint, cardboard, or code. The goal is to open myself to an encounter with something beyond myself, literally with something that is not me, in order to amplify potential outcomes. In fact, I believe that this type of collaboration with tools and materials is where innovation comes from. The key is getting to where I can meet materials on their terms, rather than wrenching them to conform with predetermined expectations.

# The Realities of Technology

Costs, access, and availability are big issues when we are working with technology in education. Not every school has budgets available for all the emerging technologies, or even for annual updates.

The world of tech moves fast. Some new and emerging tools may be outdated quickly, while others become mainstays. Choosing where to invest your educational technology resources becomes important. Here are a few elements to keep in mind as you consider which technologies to use in your STEAM work:

- Balance

    Give your learners experience with different types of technology. Working with a variety of technology types allows students to learn by comparison and contrast. By approaching the same problem with different tools, they are more likely to gain a new perspective. Developing a range of skills will also better prepare them for possible STEAM careers.

- Efficiency, Productivity, and Implementation

    Invest in tools and technologies that will get used regularly. Even if a piece of technology is amazing, if it's difficult for learners to access or implement, it likely won't be worth it in the long run. With tech, it helps to look at the big picture: better tech may sometimes cost more, but if a tool is simple to use and gets used more often, the extra expense will pay off in the long run.

- Durability and Support

    If you use a technology often, it's important that it holds up and doesn't need servicing all the time. It also makes a big difference if the tech vendor makes it easy to learn and service the technology. Nothing is worse than having an expensive piece of technology sitting broken off to the side of the room.

It's always worth investing in technology that holds up to the wear and tear of education.

## Impact

Give learners access to technology that inspires them and helps them learn. You want to choose technology that will enable them to build skill sets that will be useful in their futures.

## Research

It's not always possible to know how effective emerging technology is for education, but the best source of this knowledge is other educators. Teachers, administrators, and IT personnel are always willing to share what works well when it comes to the realities of day-to-day use. One of the benefits of social media is that trends usually tell the story. While some teachers may love a specific technology, brand, app, or device, if you look at the general trends of feedback, you'll get a clearer picture of how effective it is. You can also develop trusted sources: I know a few educators whose opinions I trust, and they often tip me off to the best new technology for STEAM learning.

## Safety, Security, and Data

Keep in mind the safety and privacy of your learners. On physical projects, safety has long been a consideration because some technology needs specialized venting, protective gear, or special power supplies. Digital safety is a growing concern, especially for younger learners; while some tech is free and convenient, it may also harvest and sell data about learners or expose them to the public online.

## Cost

Budget is often a factor in our decisions. Even the greatest technology might not make sense in many educational environments if it is not cost-effective. Educational discounts and grants can help purchase some of the more expensive technology for learning, but if those aren't available, you may need to wait for prices to drop before implementing some technology.

● The Fun Factor

Technology that excites learners is always an asset. This kind of consideration may be difficult to judge without working with learners hands-on, so it's helpful to create your own beta test with a small sampling of representative students. If the technology can be a fun and useful tool to teach and create with while also helping build your STEAM program, it's a winner.

# Makerspaces vs Creative Spaces

Many schools are incorporating makerspaces, which are areas where students can create with tools and materials. The maker mindset pairs well with STEAM and has enormous potential as a learning tool, but before you develop a makerspace, think about what will work best for your students and their projects. There are many approaches to makerspaces, from a space inside a classroom to a dedicated area of the school with its own staff. Often school makerspaces develop organically based on interest from students, teachers, and administrators. They can be in a department or based out of a school library, but the key is making sure students have access. Be open to trying out different possibilities before making commitments that might be difficult to change.

Good design is fundamental. Some makerspaces focus too much on the product and don't emphasize the conceptual understanding behind it, so it's important that the emphasis remains on the learning. If we look at professional makerspaces, design workspaces, and artist studios, we can gain some insight into ways the spaces can be organized, but when designing the space, remember to keep the focus on the learners.

A great makerspace should be inviting and have a materials library as well as readily available, accessible technology. This also requires technical elements such as power supplies and storage. Even if it's a small space, organization, design, and safety are important, as is giving the space some flexibility to grow. The space should inspire creativity as well as hands-on making and allow for the widest range of creative endeavors, including writing, designing, and making fine art.

## Building Mastery

One of the benefits of incorporating STEAM in education is that it helps learners build mastery. The interdisciplinary approach and active learning in STEAM lessons increases learners' conceptual understanding of the underlying topics as well as the learners' skill set and comfort level. Working toward mastery can itself be motivational, as author Daniel H. Pink states in his book *Drive: The Surprising Truth About What Motivates Us*: "When we make progress and get better at something, it is inherently motivating. In order for people to make progress, they have to get feedback and information on how they're doing." As an educator, we have the duty to give feedback, both conversationally and in our assessments.

This process can teach students more than the results, and the educational emphasis should always remain on the learning. To help students recognize their learning and evaluate their progress, I recommend incorporating formal and informal reflections. These reflections may seem like an unnecessary element, but they're one of the most effective ways to examine the learning as well as the creative choices and mistakes made by both the educator and the learners. Sometimes students learn important lessons, but without reflection, they might skim over them or take them for granted. It's not enough just to teach: sometimes educators need to show students what they have learned.

## Assessments

Students often focus more on their grades than their learning, and their parents may feel the same way. We do need to assess the learners and promote their self-assessments to be sure they are comprehending the material, synthesizing what they learn, and attaining mastery. To be most effective, the assessments we use should evolve with the learning and reflect major concepts and skills, as well as anecdotal learning.

This makes it necessary to design assessments around the core learning. Educators can use this need for assessments as a way of reinforcing learning and establishing priorities; whatever we hope to see in the classroom should be reflected in our assessments. Those assessments should also be designed with the students' well-being and learning in mind. Including both pre- and post-assessments can help reinforce the most important concepts that are learned and document learners' progress.

One of my biggest issues with standardized testing is that it doesn't assess creativity; in addition, research has shown that standardized testing can have negative consequences, such as causing great amounts of student stress, promoting cheating, and penalizing students unfairly. I'd recommend avoiding excessive standardized testing and instead incorporating a variety of assessments that reflect our STEAM ideology. When learning is interdisciplinary, assessments should be as well. This also helps rid assessments of the stigma of the punitive, stress-producing major exam that students fear can negatively alter their grade so that we can keep the focus on the learning.

The assessments themselves can be a teachable element that incorporates STEAM learning. There are a variety of new technological assessment tools that can make this portion of the learning process more engaging and streamlined. These include digital portfolios, reflective blogs, and testing tools that incorporate study games such as **Quizlet** (quizlet.com), **Kahoot!** (kahoot.com), **Quizizz** (quizizz.com), and **Gimkit** (gimkit.com). Another great option is asking the students to become teachers and create their own assessments and learning games. One of my favorite lessons ever was when my students collaborated to create our first smartphone app. It was a learning game for another class, and I've included it as a project extension in Part II of this book.

Students need multiple opportunities to show what they know, and the best way to do that is true project-based learning with a lot of voice and choice from the students. Partner with students to develop success criteria around the standards and then allow them time in class to do the learning and reflect along the way. This way we can know for sure what kids know and can do in their own words.

# STEAM Safety and Digital Citizenship

Although the technology used in our STEAM learning is alluring to students, it's also important to stress both physical safety—due to the potential use of electronics, chemicals, and potentially harmful materials—and virtual safety on the internet.

Physical safety is paramount in schools, so technology such as a 3D printer should be out of reach with warning signs, because it could potentially cause burns or injury if touched while printing. Some equipment, such as a laser cutter, may also need to be vented, and tools such as drones need to be registered with authorities and not flown in certain airspace. When we use chemicals of any type, it's important to take safety precautions, such as maintaining a clean workspace and potentially using eyeware and gloves, and to clean up materials thoroughly.

In terms of online safety, digital citizenship has become an essential topic to discuss with students in all subjects, but in STEAM learning it should come early, before the class becomes too active. Topics such as personal security, permissions, information sharing, privacy, online security, and basic internet etiquette are among many topics that may be considered based on the age and experience of the learners.

It also makes sense to introduce elements of media literacy when discussing digital citizenship. Students need to learn how to research and analyze information and evaluate its accuracy. There is also a question of ethics that can arise with using certain technology in terms of the data it collects and what it does with it. There are many resources on these topics which can be helpful such as the Center for Media Literacy, Common Sense Education, and National Association for Media Literacy Education. I suggest making it a project early on in which everyone participates. This can help the material have more impact, and if students add visuals to the project that can be displayed in the learning space, that will ensure it will be remembered.

## Starting Out with STEAM

If you want to implement a STEAM lesson and haven't tried it before, my advice is to think about your curriculum, identify a few key concepts, and choose one lesson that will benefit from an interdisciplinary approach that supplements what you teach now. Think about the resources you have; your first project shouldn't be a major one unless you feel confident jumping right in. Next, consider how much time you have available and what technology is at your disposal. You also want to consider your learners' strengths and interests, because when they are on board and having fun, it adds impact. I find it helpful to encourage input from the learners and engage in discourse throughout the process to assess their thinking about what's occurring.

Before you begin, think about how the STEAM project you are creating can live on after it's created by students. Is it going to be a permanent facet of the classroom? A digital asset you can share each year? Or will the students create something that they can keep? The answers to these questions will impact the design and engineering aspects of the project and may affect the student's motivation as well. Creating a legacy project that will be part of the learning environment can become an important tradition that students invest in. If it's a digital asset, consider sharing it with other educators on social media to help teach others. If your confidence level isn't high, you may want to start with a modest STEAM project, then build and improve on it in the future. This is totally acceptable; most tech products go through a beta test to find weaknesses and errors before products get released; the same idea works in education. Understand and manage your expectations if you're new to STEAM. Regardless of the choices you make, there will be a great deal of learning, but the results can and will vary.

After you've made the basic decisions, you're ready to begin. For the best results, remember to incorporate design thinking into the process. Don't be afraid to ask for feedback from other colleagues, either in your school or on social media, because you may benefit from their experience. Don't forget to document the process with photos and videos, or have a group of students document the process so you can share it and use it to reflect and to teach others later. Finally, celebrate the work and share the success and learning that occurred.

# Evolving Technology

When I was growing up, the technology available in school was a pencil, paper, and wood. I can remember using our first school computers in middle school. I'll never forget crowding around the monitor in awe the first time we installed a screensaver of hot air balloons. It's impossible to predict how technology might develop in the future, so it's essential to focus on concepts instead of teaching the technology itself. The projects we'll cover in the next section were designed with elasticity in mind, so they can be modified for different ages, skill levels, and technologies. This adaptability allows the projects to be accessible to a wide audience and to remain valuable, even as technology evolves. Remember to keep the focus on learning skills and acquiring knowledge, because the technology will change, but the STEAM mindset and process can be adapted.

Now that we've outlined the basics, it's time to explore some fun and engaging STEAM projects.

## PART II

# STEAM Projects and Technologies

· · · · · · · · · · · · · · · · · · · · · · · · · · · · ·

**I**n the following chapters, I'll share some of my favorite STEAM projects that I've used with students. I organized this section based on the technology used in the projects. Each chapter contains two projects, but there are additional projects and resources available on my website, timneedles.com.

# CHAPTER 3

# Classic Construction, Cardboard, and Upcycling

· · · · · · · · · · · · · · · · · · · · · · · · · · · · · · · · · · · · · · · · · · · · · · · · · · · · · · · · ·

**I**f you want to see creativity in action, hand a student some cardboard and glue and invite them to make something. As a kid, I used to turn cardboard boxes into rocket ships and fire engines, and as an adult, I'm inspiring others to do the same. These are the kind of projects that I post on Instagram and Twitter, and they get tons of likes because it's easy to see the creativity involved.

Classic cardboard and upcycling projects are fun, inexpensive, and easy to incorporate, regardless of your technical experience or background. If you're not familiar with the term "upcycling," it's like recycling, except rather than turning whatever is being discarded back into raw materials, we turn it instead into something new. There are an enormous number of cool, educational, and thought-provoking projects that are possible when you take materials that are no longer being used and redesign them into something with a new purpose. One of the greatest strengths of an upcycling project is that it not only inspires fun and engaging creative thinking but also models sustainable design.

As in any project, scale is also going to be a factor. It's easier to begin with something small then scale up as the students (and educators) become more comfortable with the process.

Upcycling depends on the materials you have available. When considering materials to work with, use the widest possible lens, because the best resources might literally be considered garbage by others.

I like to begin this work by presenting the materials and asking questions about them—it's necessary to think outside of the box to succeed in this arena. The artist Salvador Dalí was once served a lobster for dinner, and he pondered why he hadn't been served a telephone instead; yes, it seems absurd at first, but he then designed a lobster-telephone sculpture, one of his iconic works. What makes a lobster a lobster and a telephone a telephone? Why can't a car become an aquarium, or a train station a library? They can, of course, if we let go of our ideas about what they should be and reframe our thinking to imagine what they can be. Some of the best examples of upcycling can be found in urban areas, such as Chicago's Millennium Park, which was a parking garage that became one of the most popular public parks in the country, or the campus of Savannah College of Art and Design, where the school retrofitted many historic buildings to turn them into classrooms and workspaces for its students.

## PROJECT

## Upcycled Self-Watering Planter

This first project is to study, design, and create a self-watering planter. This can be done with a variety of different approaches, lengths of time based on the learners, and budgets, but all these variations should have no difficulty touching on all the STEAM disciplines.

A quick, popular, inexpensive approach is to use recycled materials such as a gallon soda container, which can be cut and fairly easily reconfigured to allow the mechanics to work. A more detailed approach can teach learners the science and engineering behind the process, then ask them to create their own digital rendering of a design that can be 3D printed. It's possible to push the idea even further by being more specific with the resources and costs involved; for example, ask for the project to be affordable, sustainable, and capable of being used in a greenhouse in space or on another planet, meaning that it would also need to be easily shipped and reconstructed. Bring a sense of creativity to the learning and make the project work for you and your learners.

## Project Details:

**Overview:** Design and create a self-watering or hydroponic planter out of recycled soda bottles.

**Timeline:** 45 minutes to 2 hours

**Age/Skill Level:** This project can be modified for any age and skill level

**Extended Version:** This project is for a self-watering planter, but for more advanced learners, you can assign the more difficult task of creating a true hydroponic planter that uses no soil. It uses water with a nutrient supplement, rather than the peat moss, and the roots can be supported by gravel or perlite.

## MATERIALS:

- paper and writing utensils, tablets, or computers to research, write, and draw with
- scissors
- markers
- clean, empty two-liter soda bottle
- recycled scrap piece of cotton (old socks work well)

- mixing bowl
- peat moss
- perlite
- fertilizer
- seeds (any type, but I'd start with lettuce)
- plastic wrap

**STEAM:** In this project, all the STEAM disciplines are represented equally.

**Instructions:**

1. Begin by sharing the concept and history of self-watering or hydroponic planters and exploring its uses and value for space travel, farming, and urban planting.

2. Choose which seeds you are going to plant. For beginners, I suggest lettuce, herbs, cucumbers, and tomatoes.

3. Measure the empty soda container, remove any wrappers, and cut it in half at the midpoint, leaving the cap at one end and the bottom at the other.

4. Take the cap off the bottle. Cut down the piece of cloth and place half of it in the bottle and half of it out, so it blocks the hole.

5. Mix the perlite and peat moss evenly and add some fertilizer as directed. (If the perlite and peat moss are already fertilized, you can skip this step.)

6. Pour water into the bottom portion of the bottle.

7. Turn the top part of the bottle upside down and place it into the bottom half. Make sure the cotton is in the water, it should reach at least halfway into the water to create a flow upwards toward the seeds.

8. Add one cup of your perlite mixture to the top of the bottle. You don't want it seeping through the hole with the cotton, so make sure the hole is blocked before adding the perlite.

9. Plant the seeds in the mixture. They shouldn't be too deep, approximately the length of a pen cap (which is what I have students use to create the hole in the perlite mix).

10. Very lightly water the mixture. (We use a spray bottle.)

11. Cover the planter with plastic wrap and place it in the sunlight.

12. In a few days, seeds should begin to sprout. They can then be maintained the same as any other plant.

13. Reflect on the process. Once the learners comprehend the basic process, ask them to design a more creative version of the planter with the

information they've gained. You can add additional challenges, such as creating a hanging version for classroom windows or collaborating with others to scale up the planters for a large indoor farm in an urban environment.

**14.** Share your results on social media to encourage others to do their own planting.

## Cardboard Chair Design

. . . . . . . . . . . . . . . . . . . . . . . . . . . . . . . . . . . . . . . . . . . . . . . . . . . . . . .

This project is more challenging, but it's a fantastic learning experience that touches on all the STEAM disciplines and results in some creative and innovative work. As you introduce your students to the process of designing and constructing a cardboard chair, there are some great examples to share from art and design museums, such as architect Frank Gehry's iconic cardboard chair design. The key to success is designing a chair that has both form and function: encourage your students to come up with a creative and interesting design that can also hold weight.

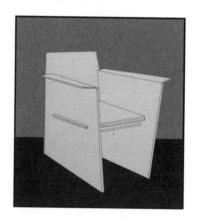

### Project Details:

**Overview:** Collaboratively design and create a chair made from cardboard that can support the weight of a person.

**Timeline:** 2 to 6 hours

**Age/Skill Level:** This project is great for more advanced learners but can be modified for any age and skill level. Learners with limited skills might try to design the chair for a stuffed animal or toy.

## MATERIALS:

- paper and drawing supplies or computers to write with
- cardboard (various weights, strengths, and sizes recommended)
- glue and/or other adhesives
- computers or smartphones with digital design software or apps
- laser cutter (optional)

**STEAM:** In this project, all the STEAM disciplines are equally represented.

**Instructions:**

1. Begin by viewing a wide variety of chairs and researching how they are designed and work structurally.

2. Brainstorm and sketch potential ideas for your cardboard chair. It should be an appealing, comfortable design and structurally sound enough to hold weight.

3. Critique the designs and choose a few to create as scale models.

4. Draw out plans for the models with precise measurements, then create the scale model.

5. Test the models for structural integrity by adding set amounts of weights at intervals and writing down the findings.

6. Review the findings and choose a final chair design to create in full scale.

7. Collaborate to create the full-size cardboard chair design.

8. Photograph the final design and videotape the weight test on the full-scale model.

9. If the weight test shows it can support the weight of a person, take safety precautions and try to sit in the chair.

10. Share the documentation and reflect on the process and results.

The classics are classic for a reason, and there is no end to the great (and inexpensive) projects that you can create with cardboard. Check out timneedles.com for more project ideas, such as creating hexaflexagons, flexagons, flextangles, and other mathematical paper toys; designing trebuchets (for pumpkin chucking); designing and creating musical instruments; building gingerbread architecture; and making magazine vases from recycled paper.

# CHAPTER 4

## Film, Video, and Animation

.......................................................

**I** have a dream that after I retire from teaching, I'll have a second career in film and television. That's how much I love this subject.

We are all surrounded by media, so working with film, video, and animation offers enormous potential for STEAM learning. In this chapter, we'll explore creating work for the various forms of video and digital screens using traditional methods, apps, and emerging digital tools. One of the benefits of working with film, video, and animation is that the work created can be easily shared and can teach others. There are many platforms for sharing the work, from student film festivals to the internet. The medium also is inherently collaborative, so students can work together to create larger works. Another plus is that in our culture we consume an enormous amount of film, video, and animation; students tend to be knowledgeable about the media and excited to learn the process and share the work. In my experience, this topic tends to unite students as they work together, and it plays to students' strengths because there are so many different roles involved.

I've seen several students so excited by working with film and video that it changed their lives and gave them a new sense of purpose. Students who were at one point underperforming in school pull it together, thanks to working in the media. Not only has it helped some students graduate but it's also become a career for former students who work in a huge range of occupations within the film industry.

This is a medium that has been evolving ever since it began in the late 1800s, and it continues to evolve today. Giving some historical perspective can be beneficial. The film industry used to be a closed profession that required a good amount of training, but technology has democratized the medium so that anyone, anywhere can create a great product. The tools are accessible, and the learning curve is quick, so it's often amazing to see what young learners can create once they learn the basics.

Thanks to new technologies, the following two projects are adaptable. Don't be deterred if you're working with a small budget or trying to create in limited circumstances: it just takes one smartphone or tablet to create. When working with film and video, it's important to consider the final product and how it might be shared; there are so many possibilities that it takes planning. Because the media is so impactful, I suggest that students create work that can help teach others in the future and support STEAM education in general. I often create smaller projects that can combine into a larger collaborative endeavor that connects with the school, community, or the larger education community. This is a great way to explore larger, more global ideas such as the environment, sustainable living, or whatever topics are prevalent in your community.

## PROJECT

## Video Poem

We'll begin with one of my favorite projects: creating a video poem. I love the creativity in this project because it can pair STEAM with English, creative writing, or foreign languages. The poem that inspires the video can be an original written by the students or it can be a poem or micro-story by another author. If you ask students to write an original poem, it allows them to do some creative writing. I've also shared some writing prompts in the Resources section. Even if you don't have students

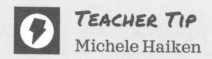

## Teacher Tip
### Michele Haiken

Poetry is about saying more with less. Word choice is key to effectively communicate a specific message. Sharing lots of models of poetry with students helps them see how poets play with format, emphasis, and word choice to create meaning.

use their own work for the video, it's always nice to have them do some writing so they connect better with the material.

The source material doesn't need to be a poem at all, as I've used the same premise with quotes from important STEAM icons. Whatever text element you use, it should be brief. The students will need to interpret the text visually. Depending on their focus, interests, and skill level, they can choose whether to include the words or show a visual interpretation of the poem. The final product can range from kinetic typography to a narrative art film.

I've found that when students are asked to creatively interpret learning from disciplines such as science, math, or engineering in the form of fine art, poems, or music, it helps them retain the information. This approach is especially successful with special education students and learners who are more visual, audial, or physical.

One of the great things about this lesson is that the resulting video poems are perfect to share on social media. I like to share them to celebrate National Poetry Month in April. A benefit of sharing during an event such as this is that while celebrating the event with great student work, it's also a way to promote both literacy and technology in education.

This version of the lesson is focused on STEAM, but it's versatile, so you can adapt it to whatever focus you want.

## Project Details:

**Overview:** Students will write a short original poem or take a poem by another author on a science theme. Possible topics include natural phenomena such as waves, seasons, the colors in the sky, or the distance to the sun. They will then add sound (music, narration, or both) and create visuals to pair with the writing as a video poem. Finally, they will design and construct a method of showing the video in a gallery type setting by creating an installation with video monitors. This isn't necessary if there isn't time, but it does implement all the STEAM disciplines, so I'll include it as a project extension. The video poems created can then be shared during National Poetry Month to support technology, art, and literacy. The lesson is centered on student choice, and technology options are outlined with examples. It is a cross-curricular lesson, so it would be great to use for art, technology, literature, writing, foreign language, or English classes.

**Timeline:** 45 minutes to 2 hours

**Ages/Skill Levels:** This project can be modified to fit all ages and skill levels.

**Extended Version:** Once the video poetry is completed, you can incorporate all the STEAM disciplines by designing and constructing a video installation. This can be achieved by upcycling older televisions and creating a sculptural work that encases them. The work of artist Nam June Paik is a great example to look at, as he combined multiple old televisions and monitors for an impact.

**STEAM:** In this project, art and technology are the predominant base topics while the science, engineering, and math components will be found in the content and themes of the writing. The extended version of the project incorporates all five subjects.

## MATERIALS:

- video camera or smartphone with video capabilities
- computers or smartphones with video editing software (Adobe Premiere Pro, Apple Final Cut Pro X, etc.)

1.  Begin with a warm-up writing activity to get the students in the right mindset for writing poetry. In the Resources section at the end of this book, I've included a link to a list of prompts, or you can make your own prompts. Allow students to write for at least five minutes before starting the activity. Some styles of poetry incorporate mathematics, such as haiku, which is constructed of three lines: the first with five syllables, the second with seven syllables, and the third with five syllables. (I find this structure is easier for students to begin with because it takes the focus off the content and puts it on the structure.) During the warm-up, I include a range of writing forms to make it more accessible to everyone.

2.  Ask the students to create or find a poem or quote they can use for their video poem. Either they can write a poem about the chosen topic (science, nature, STEAM, and so on) or they can choose a short piece of writing by someone else.

3.  Next, the students will create images to support the writing by taking photographs or shooting video clips that they can collage together. This can be done with video cameras or smartphones, but make sure the images are all the same size and orientation—either landscape (horizontal) or portrait (vertical).

4.  Import the photos or videos into a video editor either on a computer (**Adobe Premiere Pro, Apple Final Cut Pro X**, etc.) or on smartphones (**Splice, Filmmaker Pro**, etc.), then collage and edit the photos and videos into a sequence.

5.  Add the text from the poem either with words on screen, audio narration, or both.

6.  Share and critique the work.

## Educational Public Service Announcement

This project can have a big impact on the community if it is successful, and it's also a great lesson in collaboration. The project is to write, film, and edit a public service announcement based on a STEAM issue in your community. Public service announcements tend to be short, usually thirty seconds, and because this project is collaborative, it can suit almost any skill level, as long as someone in the group has the technical knowledge to film and edit.

The best part of the project is that it is a terrific opportunity to research a problem in the community, brainstorm solutions, and collaborate to create a project that has an important message. It's a great opportunity to differentiate instruction and have students work together, playing to their strengths and learning about collaboration. In the past, I've created PSAs that have aired in my school, and I've had some air on television and in local film festivals, so it's also a great opportunity to pass on the learning. Depending on how the product turns out, there may be multiple ways to reach a wider audience with an important message, but it's always a great opportunity for STEAM learning.

This is also a project in which you can create a great deal with few supplies, such as a smartphone, a green screen, and an app.

### Project Details:

**Overview:** Learners collaborate to write, film, and edit a public service announcement (PSA) focused on a STEAM-based issue in the local community. Students identify the issue and suggest solutions that they can present to viewers in a short time frame (usually thirty seconds to two minutes).

**Timeline:** 2 to 6 hours

## MATERIALS:

- paper and writing utensils or computers for writing and research
- cameras or smartphones/ devices with cameras
- computers or smartphones with digital video editing/ compositing software or apps

**Age/Skill Level:** This project can be modified for any age and skill level.

**Extended Version:** Once the PSA is created, try to get it viewed by the public to create change. Learners can brainstorm ideas for sharing the PSA and approach local television about getting it aired. They can then follow up by organizing some group activities.

**STEAM:** In this project, technology, art, and math are part of the process and all the STEAM disciplines are likely incorporated in the content and potential solutions.

**Instructions:**

1. Begin by researching STEAM issues that exist in your community, then choose a topic to focus on for your public service announcement.

2. Research and brainstorm possible solutions for the issue you chose. You may want to divide the learners into different groups to approach the topic from different perspectives.

3. Discuss ways to communicate the issue clearly to an audience in a short video. At this point in the process, it's helpful to show good examples. You can find links to some of my favorites in the Resources section.

4. Create a storyboard and draw out the most important frames of the video, accompanied by text explanations. (If you're not familiar with storyboards, there are some examples in the Resources section, but it's much like a very simple comic book.)

5. Once the concept is complete, divide the learners into different groups to collaborate on filming. There may need to be camera operators, directors, actors, lighting engineers, and sound people. I model the crew structure on those found in the film and television industry and follow the same process you might find on a professional set.

6. Film the public service announcement. It's helpful to film a few takes of each scene so there are options to choose from during editing.

7. Divide students into postproduction groups to work on editing the film, doing any special effects that might be necessary, editing the sound, and creating any necessary graphics or titles.

8. Once the groups have completed their work, view a rough cut of the public service announcement with all the learners. Discuss it and give feedback.

9. After the critique, make any changes that might be necessary.

10. Share the film and have the students organize an action campaign to get the word out about the issue and promote solutions.

Video, animation, and media arts have become the dominant art form of our time, so there are many lesson opportunities with these media. Check out timneedles.com for more project ideas, such as short documentaries, sticky note animations, kinetic typography, animated lessons, pixelations, and 8-bit animations.

# CHAPTER 5

# Digital Photography

. . . . . . . . . . . . . . . . . . . . . . . . . . . . . . . .

The magic of photography is that it allows you to see the world through the perspective of another person. If you are the photographer, it can allow you to better understand your point of view. Creating, editing, and manipulating images have great potential for STEAM learning. Digital photography tends to be an area of interest for many young learners, so the topic is naturally engaging and connects to many other subjects. We learn by seeing images, and this is an area where it's easy to touch on other subjects such as history, especially in terms of how they correspond with STEAM. It's also important to share how images can be easily manipulated to change perceptions and to add a dimension of media literacy because it can change how learners read and contextualize images.

In recent years, digital photography has changed immensely due to the growth of smartphones and the advancements and capabilities of digital cameras. Many people always have access to a digital camera, and the photographs themselves can be managed quickly; apps such as Instagram and Snapchat along with other social media platforms have changed the way we share and view images as well. These advancements have made people less precious about taking images, and learners generally have a greater knowledge of some aspects of the craft.

Even so, there is still much to be learned in this arena. While knowledge of framing and composing images has increased, other aspects such as editing, lighting, and special effects are areas of educational opportunity. I've found that if the learning offers any possibility of positively impacting a student's selfie game, they're much more likely to be invested in the project.

PROJECT

## Cyanotypes

This project is a personal favorite because it merges old-school photography techniques with new digital elements to create terrific images. The project is to create a cyanotype, most commonly referred to today as a blueprint. The process was discovered by scientist John Herschel in 1842 and has been used for centuries by scientists, engineers, designers, and artists to make reproductions. This project uses it in a way that combines all of those viewpoints.

A cyanotype is created when ferric ammonium citrate and potassium ferricyanide are combined with water and applied to a surface to make it sensitive to light. An object or negative can be placed on the coated surface, which is then exposed to light and processed with cold water to make a print. The project combines the STEAM disciplines and allows for some amazing creative experimentation, but it's also beneficial because learners can witness each step of the process and the materials are cost effective.

I use this project with all different age learners, and it has a magical quality. You don't know what you are going to get in terms of the results, but it is very fun. I suggest incorporating both contact elements (literally placing objects such as plants, scissors, toys, and more, on the treated surface) and digital negatives or blueprint designs that are printed on overhead sheets. They have a different look and can be combined to create an interesting image. I've included an extended version that is a student favorite, in which students make images of their bodies.

## MATERIALS:

- paper or cloth treated with ferric ammonium citrate and potassium ferricyanide (this can be purchased premade or prepared as part of the project)

- objects to print (leaves, cut paper, keys, etc.); anything with a unique shape and contour will work

- water

## Project Details:

**Overview:** Students create images (with or without a camera) on paper or cloth treated with the same chemical mixture used to create blueprints, a combination of ferric ammonium citrate and potassium ferricyanide.

**Timeline:** 45 minutes to 2 hours

**Age/Skill Level:** This project can be modified for any age and skill level.

**Extended Version:** I love doing a larger-scale version of this project before a holiday break or testing period by using a sheet or blanket and exposing it with the students themselves lying on it in different arrangements. To make a good exposure, the students have to lie still on the sheet in the sunlight for ten minutes, and I suggest they include some objects around them to make it clear who is who. These turn out well and become a terrific showcase of learning. You can coat the sheets with chemicals yourself or buy them ready-made, but on this scale, I'd suggest purchasing because of the amount of material used and the safety of the students.

**STEAM:** In this project, the predominant topics are science, art, and math. The technology component will be found in the camera work, and the engineering aspect can be included through the blueprint process and in the content.

**Instructions:**

1. Begin by explaining the process and history of cyanotypes.

2. Either prepare the pretreated paper or cloth (which should stay in a dark plastic bag until it is ready to be exposed), or go to the next step.

3. Making sure to take appropriate health and safety precautions, prepare the chemical compound that will make your surface light-sensitive. Combine green ferric ammonium citrate (25 grams) with 100 milliliters of water, and combine potassium ferricyanide (10 grams) with 100 milliliters of water. Combine equal parts of the two solutions, then apply the mixture to a porous surface such as paper or cloth. Be aware that these chemicals can permanently stain any surfaces, so use gloves and brushes, and cover the work area you are using.

4. Gather the materials and objects that are going to be used to make the contact print. You can use any objects with interesting silhouettes as well as oversized negatives printed out on overhead or plastic sheets. (I prepare images in photo-editing programs such as **Adobe Photoshop** by inverting the image and printing it out on acetate.)

5. Make sure there is a strong direct light source available. I prefer using sunlight, so I make the contact prints outside, but UV light works well, especially with a light box.

6. I advise doing a test print first to figure out the exposure time. Place the objects on the surface and expose the surface to the light source. Depending on the strength of your light source, the exposure time will vary from ten minutes to a few hours, but in general, about fifteen minutes is safe. Once you establish your exposure time by doing the test print, you can do any additional prints using a timer.

7. After the exposure is finished, use cold water to wash the surface and process the image. You will quickly see how well the print has turned out as it oxidizes and turns blue, but be sure to fully wash out the print.

8. Allow the print to dry by hanging it or placing it on a drying rack.

# PROJECT

## Light Painting

Another favorite photography project is light painting. This uses the magic of long-exposure photography and can be done with a camera or a smartphone and any handheld light source. It has expressive and fun results. There are some terrific historical examples from artists such as Picasso as well as numerous online video tutorials that show different techniques.

## Project Details:

**Overview:** Learners will create digital light paintings by photographing or videotaping moving light sources in a dark environment with a long shutter speed. There are a few different techniques for light painting, but the basic premise is that you have a stationary camera (or camera app on a smartphone or device) with a long shutter speed (usually the bulb setting on SLR cameras) that is shooting light sources (flashlights, LEDs, phone lights, etc.) that are moved around to "draw" an image or word.

**Timeline:** 45 minutes to 2 hours

**Age/Skill Level:** This project can be modified for any age and skill level.

**Extended Version:** Once the basic premise is understood and learners have successfully created and edited their light paintings, it's a great challenge to add more collaborators and take on a bigger light painting challenge by drawing out a large inspirational word or phrase. These are great to print and share digitally after the project is complete. It is also a terrific idea to design and engineer devices to move the lights (connect a light to string, then tether it to a pole so the light stream will become a light painting when released), such as a Rube Goldberg machine that has lights attached. It may also be interesting to create chemical compounds that glow in bottles to use as a light source.

## MATERIALS:

- cameras or smartphones/devices with cameras that have shutter speed controls (for phones, there are some specific light-painting and slow-camera apps available that are easier to use)
- handheld light sources to draw with (LEDs, smartphone lights, laser pointers, or more advanced materials that require safety precautions, such as chemical-based light sources, sparklers, steel wool, etc.)
- computers or smartphones with digital editing/compositing software or apps
- tripod or smartphone stand (optional but strongly suggested)
- black garbage bags and tape to black out windows (optional)
- timer, stopwatch, or smartphone with a timer (optional)

**STEAM:** In this project, science, technology, art, and math are the predominant topics. Engineering occurs more in the design phase and techniques.

**Instructions:**

1. Begin by explaining how long-exposure photography works and show some examples of light painting. (Some of my favorites are in the Resources section.)

2. Design the light painting. Do you want to write a word? Draw an animal? Which colors go where? Do you want to see the person holding the lights or not?

3. Depending on the number of images you want to take, it's wise to create stations so learners can rotate roles between photographing the images, painting with lights, and timing the exposure.

4. Prepare the dark space where you will create the image. (It doesn't need to be total darkness for a good image. I've created them in my classroom

by bringing down the shades, blacking out two of the five windows, and turning off the lights.)

5. Set up the camera or smartphone on a tripod, stand, or table.

6. Turn on the light sources and practice the long-exposure technique with bracketing: Fix any other variables on the camera and take a series of photographs with increasingly long exposures to see which exposure looks best. You should keep track of the exact exposure times and record the findings.

7. Once you have the correct exposure time, begin taking the images.

8. Review the images and retake any if necessary.

9. Import the images to a digital editing program or app such as **Adobe Photoshop** or **GIMP** for editing.

10. Review, critique, and share the images, then reflect on the images and learning.

These are two of my favorite photography projects, but go to timneedles.com for more project ideas, such as mixed-media photo collages, the Inside Out Project, environmental portraits, and fun with blue and green screens.

# CHAPTER 6

# Web Design, Social Media, and Podcasting

· · · · · · · · · · · · · · · · · · · · · · · · · · · ·

**T**he internet has changed the world. It's connected us, it's changed our behavior as humans, and it's still evolving. I spend my drive to work listening to podcasts, I teach daily using the web, and I'm on at least three forms of social media every day. These technologies can be huge assets to STEAM learning, but they can also be massive distractions or worse. This is why it is essential to teach these technologies and share how to use them positively. Web design includes many facets, ranging from blogging and coding to interactive web design. Social media has grown to include apps and websites, as well as audio and video formats, including podcasting and vlogging (video blogging). These forms of media can also incorporate many other crafts and technologies, such as photography, video, video games, digital drawing, radio, and virtual reality.

Web design and social media are similar in structure and design, but they function differently: websites are mostly static, while social media is entirely interactive and always changing. The two areas often interact, with websites acting as landing pads for social media, and social media pointing people toward websites. In terms of education, social media projects often unfold over a long period and are regularly updated, while web design is created once then occasionally revised or maintained.

# PROJECT

## STEAM Trading Cards

· · · · · · · · · · · · · · · · · · · · · · · · · · · · ·

This project can be a terrific teaching tool. I've done it in a variety of ways, including low-tech drawings using traditional materials, high-tech digital drawings made in programs such as Photoshop, and combinations of both, with drawn images scanned and digital text added. Once the cards are finished, they can be shared on social media or posted to a website as a permanent resource. Here are the project basics:

## Project Details:

**Overview:** Students create 2.5 x 3.5-inch trading cards based on important people in STEAM. The cards are like sports cards with an image and name on the front and a short biography, list of accomplishments, and interesting facts on the back.

**Timeline:** 45 minutes to 2 hours

**Age/Skill Level:** This project can be modified for any age and skill level.

**Extended Version:** Once the cards are created, trading them with other learners is a great way to share the learning and begin a collaboration. This is especially successful when it's long-distance or global sharing, and the STEAM cards represent regional people of note.

**STEAM:** In this project, technology and art are used specifically. All of the STEAM disciplines can be reflected in the research done on people chosen to appear on the cards.

**Instructions:**

*1.* Begin by sharing the project basics. It's helpful to show an example and include a list of important people in STEAM to choose from, though

## MATERIALS:

- paper and writing utensils, tablets, or computers to research, write, and draw with
- computers or smartphones with digital editing and compositing software or apps
- scissors, colored pencils, and drawing tablets (optional)

students don't have to be limited to that list. In the Resources section, I've included my Quizlet list of STEAM influencers

2. Invite students to choose an important STEAM person to research and create a card for.

3. Ask the students to research their STEAM influencer and write a short biography and a list of five major accomplishments. They should also find a photo of their STEAM influencer as a reference.

4. Students will draw their STEAM influencer, either on paper or on a digital editing program such as **Adobe Photoshop** or **GIMP**. Students not comfortable with drawing portraits can trace the reference photo and color it.

5. Students design the card. It should have the STEAM influencer's portrait and name on the front, with the biography and list of accomplishments on the back.

6. Print and cut out sets of the STEAM cards and use them as a study guide and resource.

7. Share digital versions of the cards on social media, or make a website to show them.

Web design can be a great summative element in this project because it can combine so many of the other STEAM elements and can show what the students learned. When the cards are archived on a website, they can live on and continue to teach. The website is not only a reflective tool but also an aid to future learners.

Before working with websites and social media, it is key to review internet safety and media literacy. Some schools don't allow students to interact online without authorization, but even if your ultimate creations won't appear live on the internet, it is important to teach students how to navigate online and filter information. Even when the security must be high due to the age or culture of the learners, meaningful work can still be done.

Next, we'll move on to podcasting, vlogging, and radio. These may not seem like forms of social media, but they can be, especially as the genre expands to include apps such as **SoundCloud**, **Voxer**, and **Spotify**.

When I first heard about educators using podcasting with students, I didn't understand how they were incorporating the media. To learn more, I began listening to podcasts such as *This American Life* and *Radiotopia*, and I became enamored with the medium. I found myself listening to numerous podcasts on my drive to and from work each day. When one of my favorite podcasts, *Third Coast*, announced they were holding a podcasting competition and that the winners would be played on the radio, I knew I had to enter. The problem was that I had no idea how to create a podcast, or even what tools to use. This was before the podcasting boom, so resources were not readily available. I ended up using my phone to record and some freeware (**Audacity**) to edit; I felt that if the narrative was strong enough, it would make up for any technical weaknesses. It worked well: I ended up being a finalist in the competition, and my story was played on their show.

I was so excited about having created an audio narrative that I wanted to bring that experience into my class. I searched for other opportunities that might be good motivation for my students, and I found a terrific podcast called *StoryCorps*. It features personal stories from people of all backgrounds that often have some

**Teacher Tip**
Michele Haiken

. . . . . . . . . . . . . . . . . . . . . . . . . . . . . . . . . . . . . . . . . . . . . . .

Film and podcasting allow students to enhance writing with visual and audio formats.

historical or social significance and help build empathy and understanding. The compelling and educational stories available range from firsthand accounts of the families of September 11 victims, to military experiences, to love stories from around the world. *StoryCorps* also offers an app, which enables people to do their own interviews. The app facilitates the recording process, offers sample questions, and allows users to upload their audio interview to the *StoryCorps* archives if they choose to.

Each Thanksgiving, *StoryCorps* has an annual program focused on interviews recorded with friends and family, especially older people. That program gave me the inspiration for the next project, in which students record their own podcast interview.

## PROJECT

## STEAM Podcast Interview

. . . . . . . . . . . . . . . . . . . . . . . . . . . . . . . . . . . . . . . . . . . . . . . .

When we ask students to share a personal, meaningful story from their lives, it can be challenging. Telling a personal story could be a terrific project for the right person with the right story, but younger learners haven't amassed that many stories, and nearly all learners might wrestle with some of the fear of judgment that we touched on earlier. Interviewing someone they know well is almost always an easier place to begin. When we ask learners to have a conversation with an older loved one and ask them about important moments in their lives, the conversation itself often becomes a memorable moment. Giving students a chance to ask these questions offers them an opportunity to engage in a conversation that they might not have had otherwise.

These conversations could be with anyone, from friends and relatives to you, their teacher. The best scenario for this interview would be with a relative or an alumnus who has done some work in STEAM, but as an educator, you are fair game as well. I've had students interview me for this project, and although it's never exactly what I expected, it's always an interesting learning experience. I would remind you that students, especially younger ones, might not filter their thoughts or questions; there's a chance you might be asked something that you are not expecting and need to be diplomatic or give the question some thought, which is not a problem.

## Project Details:

**Overview:** Based on the *StoryCorps* model, students will create a short audio podcast of an interview relating to STEAM.

**Timeline:** 1 to 3 hours

**Age/Skill Level:** This project can be modified for any age and skill level.

**Extended Version:** A great extension to this project is submitting the interview podcasts to *StoryCorps* and sharing them with the world. Students can also create a series of interviews that are connected thematically and can be used by other educators.

**STEAM:** In this project, technology is part of the process, and all the STEAM disciplines are likely incorporated in the interview content.

## Instructions:

1. Begin by watching and listening to *StoryCorps* interviews created by young learners.

2. Find STEAM interviewees and research their backgrounds. The interviews can be done by individuals, small groups, or the entire class. Interview subjects can be family members, friends, teachers, retired professionals, local businesspeople, or experts found and interviewed through the internet or social media.

3. Adapt sample questions that *StoryCorps* provides in their app and research good questions to ask, then add your own questions to prepare for the interview.

4. Do a mock interview where learners can test the sound recording by interviewing each other.

5. Record the interview with the STEAM subject.

6. Edit the interview if necessary.

7. Share and upload the interview on social media or in the *StoryCorps* archive if you want others to hear it (optional).

8. Reflect on the interview and what was learned in the process.

Social media and the web are always evolving, so opportunities are endless with these technologies. Check out timneedles.com for more project ideas, such as STEAM blogging, interactive web design, web-based art, The Sketchbook Project, Global Nomads, and 36 Days of Type.

# CHAPTER 7

## Coding

. . . . . . . . . . . . .

*I*t's incredible what you can create in the classroom today with a simple knowledge of code. Computer science was once a specialty subject, but working with code is an important skill for everyone in the future and one of the foundational elements of STEAM learning. Technology has made working with code in educational settings much easier, regardless of the age or skill level of the learners. Students who have no background in coding can learn the basics from languages such as Blockly, which is used in tools such as **Code.org** and **Scratch** to make coding easy and fun to learn. There are many different coding languages, each has its strengths and purposes; make sure you touch on some of the most popular and accessible coding languages and share why they are useful.

In many ways, learning to code is like learning a foreign language, but in coding there are consistent principles that apply across many languages. When students are exposed to the fundamentals of code syntax and structure early, coding is often easier for them to learn because they can apply those fundamentals to the various languages. Thanks to the availability of languages such as Blockly, educators have been teaching elements of coding to students at younger ages, so working with code is much more natural to them. As with learning a language, some learners may take to coding quickly while others struggle; using a variety of approaches and techniques will give options to learners at all levels.

I like to introduce code with short projects that deliver different skill sets each month, then culminate in larger projects later in the year. This offers a greater diversity of STEAM activities and allows learners time to process what they've learned. It also allows students who might not have totally grasped the lessons to have more time to practice and gain competency before we move forward in our learning. How you choose to apply these types of projects will be based on the audience you're working with, the accessibility of the technology, and your educational priorities.

In teaching coding over the years, I've learned that the learning curve is shrinking; students are moving through the projects faster. Because of that, I've encouraged my students to take on larger projects with more impressive results, including coding apps, robots, video games, computer art, artificial intelligence, and interactivity. When working with coding in education, it helps to have lofty goals because you often accomplish them. It's important to introduce students to technologies and concepts such as exploring global warming solutions through artificial intelligence and planetary engineering and terraforming on Mars because even though they may seem out of reach now it may be their reality in the future.

**PROJECT**

WHEN RUN → REPEAT
MOVE FORWARD → | PIXEL

## Code Art

. . . . . . . . . . . . . . . . . . . . . . . . . . . . . . . . . . .

Your students' abilities and knowledge will shape what you can do when teaching coding, but I like to begin with a series of small sequential projects. This first project is a great one because it allows students to be as technically advanced as they wish. It can be done by someone new to coding or by a pro, and it will be successful either way. The project is to create a work of coding art—basically, a digital drawing that can repeat on a monitor. This can be accomplished in many ways by using technology such as **Scratch** or **Code.org**, as well as by working in more advanced coding languages.

## Project Details:

**Overview:** Create art based in coding. It can be simple repeating line art or more complex interactive art, but the key is that it is driven by code.

**Timeline:** 45 minutes to 2 hours

**Age/Skill Level:** This project can be modified for any age and skill level.

**Extended Version:** After the basic art coding is complete, design a way to show it by creating a stand with monitors. It's also an interesting challenge to create a more immersive code art experience that can be shared through an app or website.

**STEAM:** In this project, all the STEAM disciplines are covered evenly based on the choices you make.

**Instructions:**

1. Begin by assessing the learners' skills in coding. If they are new to coding, some preliminary lessons with a Blockly-based program such as **Code.org** are helpful. If they are more advanced, they can explore different examples of code-based art online before choosing an approach.

2. Choose a creative concept and map a pathway to achieving the idea through coding. Learners who have limited skills or are new to code can

create the entire project with the Artist Lesson on **Code.org** (studio.code.org/s/artist); intermediate learners can create the code art using Scratch; and more advanced learners can use any of the coding languages to create their code art.

3. Begin coding the project. The coding time will depend upon the choices made for the project, so it can vary widely.

4. Beta test the code, fix any errors that may prevent the programs from working, and make any aesthetic or creative changes necessary.

5. Share your code-based art with each other and online, and reflect on the process and what was learned.

## Video Games

This project is always a favorite. Gaming culture has become enormous, so young learners respond well to this project and create a wide assortment of games. To avoid violent games and set expectations, it may be necessary to set some parameters before the project begins. I always love gauging the interest level of each student and helping them achieve their goals for the games because it can be a great learning experience. I also add the extra motivator of video game competitions to help give direction to the work the students are doing and give them a place to share their games.

### Project Details:

**Overview:** Students create a video game.

**Timeline:** 2 to 12 hours (depending on the complexity of the video game)

## MATERIALS:

- computers, tablets, or smartphones with access to coding tools
- video game controllers, headphones, and viewers (optional)

**Age/Skill Level:** This project can be modified for any age and skill level.

**Extended Version:** You can push the STEAM element further by creating your own controller with a **Makey Makey** input. There are also several video game design competitions for students that are terrific to help motivate students through the process of creating a game. My favorites are Games for Change, The National STEM Video Game Challenge, and the Scholastic Art and Writing Awards. These competitions are perfect for students who are interested in gaming and want to build their skills and take on a challenge. It's also great to create your own local competition with prizes to motivate students. The best extended challenge is to create a video game based on teaching and make it into an app that can be used by other students.

**STEAM:** In this project, all the STEAM disciplines are equally represented.

**Instructions:**

1. Begin by exploring the types of video games that are possible and researching what variables are necessary to create them. It's a good idea to share video games created by students to set expectations and inspire the learners.

2. Do warm-up coding activities that will build the specific skills learners will need to create their game. This will be based on the skill level of the learners; for learners new to coding, a program such as **Scratch** would be appropriate.

3. Design and draw any characters or objects needed for the game. I begin by using traditional supplies such as pencils and paper, then use a digital drawing program to finalize them.

4. If the characters or objects need to be animated, you can import the drawing into a program such as **Adobe Photoshop** or **Piskel** (piskelapp.com) to create simple GIF animations.

5. Code the game itself. This could be an individual or collaborative effort, depending on the grade level and timeline.

6. Once the basic code is written, import the characters and any animations into the game and write the key instructions.

7. Beta test the games by having students share them with friends and fill out a rubric with feedback for changes and alterations. (An example is provided in the Resources section.)

8. Fix any bugs or errors in the game.

9. Create titles and credits for the game and add them into the code.

10. Once the game is complete, share it with others. Complete the rubric again, then reflect on the game and the learning.

Coding is one of the most important skills of the future, so check out timneedles.com for more project ideas such as programming robots with code, coding video and photography filters, and coding to create apps.

# CHAPTER 8

## Digital Drawing and Design

· · · · · · · · · · · · · · · · · · · · · · · · · · · · · · · · · · · · · · · · · · · · · · ·

**I**'m an artist who loves drawing, but even if you approach the subject with some trepidation, new technologies have expanded the world of drawing and made it much more accessible. Some of my favorite digital drawing and painting projects incorporate great design fundamentals as well as STEAM learning. There are many technological options available for digital painting and drawing. Many learners enjoy using a drawing tool or tablet, whether it's drawing on a device such as an iPad or Wacom tablet or using a smartphone app such as **Photoshop, Clip Studio Paint, Procreate, Paper, Autodesk SketchBook,** or one of the many others out there. This medium is expressive and versatile and allows learners to explore their imagination and creativity. When working with digital drawing and painting, I find it helpful to critique work as a class because there are so many teachable moments that occur. It allows students to learn from each other, and they also develop the skill of discussing and examining their work and that of others in a meaningful way.

Some learners may be excited about digital drawing, while others may resist it. Be mindful of how you present this subject, because the way educators frame these projects can have a huge effect on their students. I encourage educators to work alongside students and do their own drawings. It's always important for educators to model activities, but it may be even more impactful in this area: if educators present a belief that they aren't able to draw but they show a willingness and excitement to learn, it gives students license to do the same.

# Digital Self-Portrait

. . . . . . . . . . . . . . . . . . . . . . . . . . . . . . . . . . . . . . . . . . . .

Every year, the first digital drawing project I have my students do is a self-portrait. I define "self-portrait" broadly because not everyone is comfortable with their image; students can incorporate different elements into their portraits, such as words, colors, and textures, and I suggest they be open to repeating elements as well.

## Project Details:

**Overview:** Learners will design and create a unique digital self-portrait incorporating photography, drawing, and type. They will build their digital drawing and design skills while expressing themselves in a creative portrait.

**Timeline:** 2 to 4 hours

## MATERIALS:

- paper and drawing supplies or computers for writing and drawing
- cameras or smartphones/ devices with cameras
- computers or smartphones with digital editing/ compositing software or apps

**Age/Skill Level:** This project can be modified for any age and skill level.

**STEAM:** In this project, technology and art are the predominant topics. The other disciplines are based on the student's interests and inspirations.

**Instructions:**

1. Begin by either photographing each learner or inviting students to take a self-portrait photograph to work from. They can take one image or numerous photographs.

2. Invite the students to write about themselves and their recent experiences. (I do this project at the beginning of the year, so I usually have the students write about their summer.) The writing should fill a full page and can either be written traditionally on paper and then scanned/photographed or written directly on a computer. If the students run out of content, you can have them freewrite or repeat elements.

3. Invite the students to draw themselves using the photograph(s) as reference.

4. Once the drawing is complete, students can collage aspects of the photograph, drawing, and writing together. Invite them to be creative and try to represent their personality. This aspect of the project can be in color or black and white and be completed either digitally or traditionally using printouts and glue.

5. Share the final images and invite the students to write a short reflection about what they learned and how the image they created represents them.

## PROJECT

## STEAM Infographics

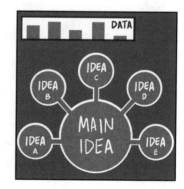

This project, to create an infographic explaining a STEAM principle, teaches important skills, requires collaboration, and results in work that can be used to teach others. In introducing the project, I invite my students to research STEAM concepts they find most interesting, but I also give them a list of topics that might help other students the most. To make my list, I begin by considering the principles I most want learners to comprehend; I then think about the things my learners are having the most difficulty with. Cross-referencing those two lists, I create my topic list, which students can choose from to make their infographic. After the infographics are created, I post them in my classroom, and they go on to aid learners for years.

## Project Details:

**Overview:** Students design and create an infographic that visually explains an important STEAM principle. Learners choose a concept in science, technology, engineering, art, or math and illustrate it with digital drawings and written explanations.

**Timeline:** 2 to 5 hours

**Age/Skill Level:** This project can be modified for any age and skill level.

**STEAM:** In this project, technology and art are used directly, while all the STEAM disciplines can appear as content.

**Instructions:**

1. Begin by examining different infographics and taking note of what elements are most informative and communicate the ideas clearly.

## MATERIALS:

- paper and writing utensils or computers for writing, drawing, and research
- computers, tablets, or smartphones with digital editing/compositing/drawing software or apps, such as Adobe Photoshop, Adobe Illustrator, Canva, or Google Charts

2. The infographic can be created individually or collaboratively. If this is going to be done as a group project, set up the groups.

3. Each person or group chooses a STEAM topic for their infographic. The topics should be science, technology, engineering, art, or math concepts that are important to learn and remember. Examples might include parts of a cell, a keyboard shortcut for a program, the ISTE Standards for Students, PEMDAS (parentheses, exponents, multiplication, division, addition, subtraction), pi, and so on.

4. Once the topic is chosen, write out the most important elements that need to be covered and what types of images might be helpful.

5. Consider the dimension and structure of the infographic. Is it vertical or horizontal? Does the content emanate from the center, move from top to bottom, or have some other flow?

6. Draw a thumbnail version of the design to work toward for the final version.

7. Create any visual elements or icons needed for the infographic. Use a digital drawing program or hand draw the images, then scan them.

8. After the graphics and icons are created, use a digital editing program to lay them out and combine them with any necessary background elements.

9. Choose a clear and direct font and add the text elements to the image.

10. Complete the infographic with a title and critique it to see if it clearly illustrates the STEAM concept.

11. Make any necessary revisions. Print the infographic and also share it online to pass on the learning. Finally, hang up the final infographic and reflect on the process.

Check out timneedles.com for more project ideas, such as creating e-comics, quote portraits, digital illustration, and type drawings.

# CHAPTER 9

# 3D Design, Printing, and Construction

· · · · · · · · · · · · · · · · · · · · · · · · · · · · ·

Technologies such as 3D printing and laser cutting still really impress me, and I feel like they are loaded with potential. I see amazing STEAM learning occur when my students explore the emerging technologies of fabrication, modeling, industrial design, and manufacturing with tools such as laser cutters, CNC machines (computer prototyping and manufacturing), vacuum forming, and 3D printing.

Many projects in these areas utilize similar techniques with different technologies, so you can use whatever is at your disposal. If you are creating a mold, for example, it could be done in a 3D printer, a vacuum former, an actual mold maker, or created by hand—all with similar results. In this chapter, we'll cover STEAM projects that can be created by technology-aided cutting, burning, modeling, machining, etching, carving, milling, and molding.

The design process is going to come into play more in these projects because there are generally greater costs in terms of both time and money. To be efficient, work out the details of projects before you begin the creation stage. It always helps to build models before producing a final result.

3D printing may also be one of the most discussed yet underutilized technologies in education. While the technology has tremendous potential for STEAM learning as well as in the professional world, it has met with some resistance in education. Part of the issue is that many 3D printers were spread throughout classrooms around the world often before teachers were fully trained and knew how to use them in a meaningful way. This resulted in a ton of cookie-cutter 3D-printed projects made with the earliest versions of printers; disappointed by the results, many teachers rejected the technology. This technology is too useful and important to deny it to students, so we want to make sure we are focused on creative projects that use it well.

Before I began teaching 3D printing, it appeared complicated and difficult, but the learning curve was easy, especially with the right printers, apps, and programs. It's important not to reduce the use of this technology to simply outputting 3D prints of 3D designs. Even though 3D design and 3D printing are related, they are different and require different skills. 3D design can serve a variety of purposes aside from 3D printing; it can allow you to previsualize designs, build virtual worlds, or explore ideas in a 3D sketchbook. Even if you don't have a 3D printer available, you can still do amazing work with 3D design. However, 3D printers have become more affordable because of their popularity, and the other technologies seem to be following suit. When using 3D printing, I advocate investing in a few different tools because it gives students more experience and versatility. I'll often use more than one app or program with learners and base my choices on the needs of the project and skill sets of students.

# PROJECT

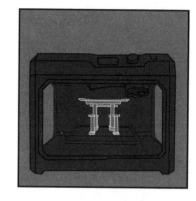

## 3D Architecture

In this project, students create an architectural work. Depending on your learners and their abilities, it could be a simple imaginary house or a more advanced skyscraper that is true to scale. The great thing about this project is that it effortlessly incorporates all the disciplines of STEAM, from designing a structure that will stand and resist earthquakes to creating a work with a beautiful and creative form.

## Project Details:

**Overview:** Create and 3D print a 3D architectural design for a real-life location. This project allows students to design and create a scale model for their architectural design, based on an actual place they have researched.

**Timeline:** 2 to 6 hours

**Age/Skill Level:** This project can be modified for any age and skill level.

**Extended Version:** It may be possible to build the design in the real world. In the past I have had students design for communal areas within the school, then bring their designs to fruition, thanks to grants.

## MATERIALS:

- cameras or smartphones/ devices with cameras
- computers or smartphones with 3D design and digital
- editing/compositing software or apps
- paper and drawing supplies
- 3D printer or laser cutter

**Instructions:**

1. Research architectural design and the choices architects make to combine structural engineering and creativity. Show examples such as Frank Lloyd Wright, who was inspired by natural settings, or Frank Gehry or I.M. Pei, whose buildings stand out from their surroundings.

2. Choose a location to use as a site for the structure and invite students to research the area as they begin thinking of a design.

3. Sketch a design either in pencil or digitally on a digital drawing program such as **Adobe Photoshop**.

4. Have students examine each other's designs and give feedback.

5. Begin the architectural design in a 3D design program such as **Tinkercad**, **Morphi**, **SketchUp**, **Blender**, or **AutoCAD**.

6. When the design is complete, prepare it for 3D printing. While printing is occurring, invite learners to take screenshots of their designs and use a photo editing program such as **Adobe Photoshop** or **GIMP** to insert an image of their structure into the location it was designed for.

7. Print the photo composite of the design and display it with the final 3D-printed version for a class critique.

## PROJECT

# 3D Fashion Design

Designing and creating a 3D-printed or fabricated garment is one of the most creative learning experiences with this technology. Using 3D tools to create on-demand fashion is one of the most interesting recent technological advancements, and there are amazing examples to share with learners: Danit Peleg's customizable 3D-printed clothing, threeASFOUR's 3D-printed runway dresses, Anouk Wipprecht's Spider Dress 2.0, and Sylvia Heisel's Names Dress, which is a tribute to the women of STEAM. When choosing a garment, consider the learners' interest and knowledge level as well as their skill set. Creating a scarf would be fairly simple; a skirt would be great for more intermediate learners. Advanced learners might take on a full dress or jacket.

## Project Details:

**Overview:** Create simple and creative fashion designs from repeated, interlocking 3D-printed shapes. 3D-printed fashion is a wave of the future, and this project is focused on creating a simple garment that shows its potential and teaches the basic principles.

**Timeline:** 2 to 6 hours

**Age/Skill Level:** This project is ideal for more skilled learners, but it can be adjusted to fit younger learners or learners new to the process by scaling the goal down to creating a garment for a toy or stuffed animal.

**Extended Version:** It is a terrific challenge to take this concept to the next level by tackling a more complex 3D-printed garment, such as a dress or jacket. A large project like this works well collaboratively, and there have been notable examples that can provide inspiration. There are also some terrific resources available from the Cooper Hewitt Design Museum and the Museum of Arts and Design.

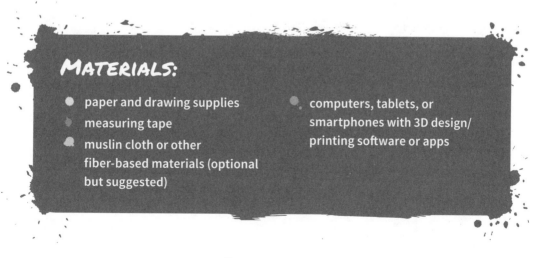

## MATERIALS:

- paper and drawing supplies
- measuring tape
- muslin cloth or other fiber-based materials (optional but suggested)
- computers, tablets, or smartphones with 3D design/printing software or apps

**Instructions:**

1. Share examples of 3D-printed clothing and fashion designs and choose the type of garment you want to create.

2. Draw out a sketch of the project you want to create and the 3D-printed material you will create. The 3D-printing materials should be able to be linked together, whether they are interlocking shapes or literally fused or printed together; you can brainstorm this aspect together.

3. Consider what material you are going to 3D print with—flexible plastics work best—and whether you will weave fibrous materials in between the 3D-printed materials.

4. Take any necessary measurements using the tape measure.

5. Create a pattern incorporating the measurements.

6. Create a sample garment from muslin to use as a model (optional).

7. Design the digital 3D-printable materials using a 3D design program on a computer or tablet.

8. Print out the 3D material and fuse or interlock, if necessary.

9. Use the pattern to assemble the 3D-printed parts of the garment.

10. Have someone try on the garment and check the measurements to see if any adjustments are necessary.

11. Make any necessary alterations and complete the garment.

12. Photograph the final product, share the photos, and reflect on the process and learning.

These two 3D design and construction projects are just the beginning. Check out timneedles.com for more ideas, including projects on 3D casting, 3D art history works, STEAM vinyl toy designs, creating sculptures from drawings, industrial design, laser-cut drawings, 3D maps, laser-cut jewelry, and 3D-printed food molds.

# CHAPTER 10

## Robotics and Drones

· · · · · · · · · · · · · · · · · · · · · · · · · · · · · · · · ·

**R**obots are cool. They were cool when I was growing up; they were cool in films such as *Short Circuit* in the '80s, and they even remained cool after trying to kill Will Smith in *I, Robot* in the new millennium. There is something inherently compelling about robotics, and our world has continued to incorporate robots into more and more industries. In this chapter, we'll explore using robots and drones (flying robots) in education. There are many ways to use robots and drones in the classroom, from designing robot/drone mazes, to interactive coding robots, to creating your own robot or drone—all of which lead to terrific STEAM learning. In addition to classroom learning, more and more schools have robotics teams that compete in events worldwide, adding new dimensions and opportunities for your learners.

Whenever possible, it's beneficial to have students build their own robot. This may sound like a complicated process, but it doesn't need to be. There are simple prefabricated robots and robot kits that can be constructed in a short time and will help teach learners how the components work. This type of project can be built with younger students to give them a base knowledge they can build on through their school years. For more experienced students, there are more advanced robotics supplies and kits. There is already a huge range of robotics tools available for education, and it seems that each year more are added into the mix.

# Random Drawing Robot

. . . . . . . . . . . . . . . . . . . . . . . . . . . . . . . . . . . . . . . . .

This project requires either a simple robot or readily available materials that can be hacked to make one. The goal is to create a random drawing robot, and it's always fun.

## Project Details:

**Overview:** Design and build a simple random drawing robot. This can be done from scratch, from a robot kit, or by hacking other technology. The robot should be able to move randomly with drawing or painting supplies attached; the random movement can be programmed, or it can be caused by giving the robot no directional instructions.

**Timeline:** 45 minutes to 3 hours

**Age/Skill Level:** This project can be modified for any age and skill level.

## MATERIALS:

- paper
- drawing supplies
- rubber bands
- glue (optional)
- cameras or smartphones/devices with cameras

- robot (Based on the time available and the learner's skill level, this can be built from scratch, assembled from a kit such as National Geographic or littleBits, or hacked from other technology. See the Resources section for links to specific examples.)

**Extended Version:** After building a random drawing robot, learners can take on the more advanced challenge of designing, coding, and creating an intentional drawing robot that draws based on either coded commands or inputs conveyed through a controller.

**STEAM:** All the STEAM disciplines are represented equally in this project.

**Instructions:**

1. Choose a robot to work with and build the robot collaboratively. It's best if learners take part in each aspect of this project but are divided into groups with different responsibilities based on their interests and strengths.

2. Once the robot is ready and working, brainstorm collaboratively and design a way to attach the drawing supplies.

3. Test the robot's ability to draw and solve any problems that arise.

4. Once the robot is ready and the drawing supplies are attached, demonstrate it working and celebrate the success. I suggest you let it run for at least five minutes to create a denser drawing and see if you can mathematically predict its movement in any way.

## Drone Photography

Drones have become more common and are now used for many different purposes, from delivering packages to filming commercials to serving as the visual centerpiece in live concerts. They are a bit misunderstood by the mass public, and I find there is some trepidation about them. However, at my school, we now have our annual faculty photo taken with a drone, and they have proven to be a valuable resource.

## MATERIALS:

- drone kit complete with camera
- computers, tablets, or smartphones with digital editing/compositing software or apps
- basic tool kit (screwdrivers, tape, glue, etc.)
- bright, large material to create a design on the ground (cloth, blankets, cardboard, etc.)

This is one of the best drone projects I have worked with. Students build a drone and use it to photograph an aerial image. The project can be done with inexpensive drones or more complex and challenging ones; make your choice based on your learners (as well as regional and national drone laws). Also keep in mind that when working with drones, there may be challenges depending on the state where you live and the physical environment where you'll be flying the drone.

## Project Details:

**Overview:** Build a simple drone with a camera and use it to take an aerial photograph of a design on the ground.

**Timeline:** 45 minutes to 2 hours

**Age/Skill Level:** This project is best for advanced learners but can be modified for learners with more limited skills by skipping the building process and using a small drone.

**STEAM:** In this project, all the STEAM disciplines are equally represented.

**Instructions:**

1. Research drones, exploring the different types and how the technology is being used now and may be used in the future.

2. Collaborate to assemble your drone. Examine the parts and take notes on how the technology works in the process. (Many possible drones could be used for this project, ranging from simple, inexpensive models that can be put together in an hour to more expensive and complex drones that may require special Federal Aviation Administration (FAA) paperwork. The choice is dependent upon the learners, the time available, and the legal restrictions in your area.)

3. After the drone is assembled, brainstorm a design that you can photograph from the drone. Examples could be an inspiring word or a symbol of the class or school.

4. Use math to calculate how large the design needs to be for the estimated height of the drone.

5. Choose materials that you can lay out on the ground to photograph from above. It's wise to use materials that are easy to clean up and organize, as well as earth-friendly.

6. Lay out the design to be photographed.

7. Use the drone to photograph the image. Make sure to take all necessary safety precautions: it may not be wise to include students in the image, depending on the type of drone and the location where it will be flying.

8. Land the drone and download the image.

9. Edit the image to add text if necessary, then share and reflect on the learning.

I believe that robots are the future. Use them well, and you will see some engaged learners. For more project ideas, such as student inventions, robot coding, hacking robots, and robot and drone obstacle courses, check out timneedles.com.

# CHAPTER 11

## Augmented and Virtual Reality

· · · · · · · · · · · · · · · · · · · · · · · · · · · · · · · · · · · · · · · · · · · · · · · · · ·

**A**ugmented reality and virtual reality (AR/VR) are two of the most powerful technologies for education that we will discuss, and the tools are progressing quickly. The power of this technology is its ability to transport students anywhere in the universe and to show rather than tell. It also allows learners to explore interactive learning at their own pace, which is enormously powerful. I've met educators from around the world who are doing exciting things with AR/VR, but I believe we are only grazing the surface of these tools' enormous potential.

I've never had more fun with technology than I did when drawing in a virtual space using the **Google Tilt Brush** (tiltbrush.com). For me, it was a ground-breaking moment, and it gave me a glimpse of what is possible. Anyone, anywhere can use AR/VR to teach. It doesn't need to be cost-prohibitive because you can transport students on a virtual field trip using only a smartphone and a cardboard viewer.

As with most technology, AR/VR requires a period of discovery and exploration as we learn how to best implement it. Our advantage in today's age is that we can connect with other users and share our experiences with tools such as AR/VR. The tools to view and create AR/VR vary in sophistication, cost, and quality, and there are programs and resources available that can be helpful for someone who is beginning with the technology.

A great way to begin exploring virtual reality is by looking at STEAM careers that use it in the real world. Several videos give students a behind-the-scenes look at the different occupations and what they entail; these can be inspiring, but they can also potentially intimidate students, so it's important to include a conversation in which students give feedback on what they learned and how they felt. It's also helpful to familiarize students with the technology itself before interacting with it because that first experience might be new, and you don't want to potentially create a negative association.

Another terrific way to start using virtual and augmented reality is to reinforce learning by adding an interactive experience. As an example, if you're teaching a lesson about space, it would be great to give students a firsthand look at what it's like on the space station. These kinds of interactive experiences can be powerful and give students a new perspective on their learning; they also allow students to experience things that might not be possible otherwise. There are numerous resources available for educators with little to no experience in AR or VR that can give students an engaging and interesting experience.

Once learners have engaged with augmented and virtual reality, the next step is creating their own AR or VR experience. Here, cost can make a big difference in the ease and intensity of the process and the quality of the finished work. It's generally easier and more cost-effective to begin with augmented reality because apps such as **Quiver**, **Morphi**, and **Just a Line** let students build and see their creation in augmented reality in minutes, without needing to learn how triggers or other technical elements work.

## Augmented Reality Career Exploration

There are many different ways to introduce AR/VR, but I like to incorporate a lesson in which students become the teachers. A great example is this project, in which students do research and then create a poster that includes a related augmented reality image. The project is flexible and can be altered to fit the learner's skill level.

### Project Details:

**Overview:** Learners will research a STEAM career and create a poster to share what they have learned with others; the poster will include an augmented reality image. Depending on a student's skill level, this image can be a simple photograph that combines multiple elements (for example, if a student is researching a paleontologist, they could create a self-portrait with a dinosaur added to the image) or, if the students are more advanced, the poster can include trigger images that cause augmented-reality images to appear. (In the paleontologist example, the poster viewed through an augmented reality app might cause a dinosaur to materialize.)

### MATERIALS:

- cameras or smartphones/devices with cameras
- computers or smartphones with augmented reality and digital editing/compositing

software or apps such as Quiver, Morphi, Augment, 3DBear, Just a Line, HP Reveal, Artivive, and CoSpaces

**Timeline:** 45 minutes to 3 hours

**Age/Skill Level:** This project can be modified for any age and skill level.

**STEAM:** Technology and art are the predominant topics. Other disciplines may be represented, depending on which career a student decides to research.

**Instructions:**

1. Introduce the project and explain that students will teach each other about STEAM careers while building skills in augmented reality technology. Show an example of the augmented reality format you are going to use. Share a list of STEAM careers that students can choose to research, but tell students they can explore careers that aren't represented on the list.

2. Invite each learner to choose a career to explore, but try to have every learner research a different career so there is more learning. If two students are hoping to research the same career, see if there is a way to differentiate the careers with details. (For example, if they both want to research a designer, break it into a fashion designer and a web designer.)

3. Students research and take notes on the career, including what skills are involved and what education is necessary. They collect images that might be good to use for the augmented reality image.

4. When the learners have amassed enough knowledge on the occupation, they can organize the data and design the poster by laying out facts in a digital design program.

5. Learners choose an image to augment. They either add to the image so that it includes visual elements in addition to those found in reality, or they import the image into an augmented reality program and create a trigger and image for the poster.

6. Learners complete the poster design by adding the augmented reality image. Print the poster.

7. When the posters are all complete, they should be shared and posted around the learning space as a resource. They can also be shared on social media to help teach others about STEAM careers.

8. Reflect on what has been learned and assess students' interest in different STEAM careers. This data may help the educator select future projects.

# PROJECT

## Virtual Reality Drawing

. . . . . . . . . . . . . . . . . . . . . . . . . . . . . . .

Learning augmented reality can help students build the skills they need to progress into working with virtual reality, which is more immersive and often more costly and challenging. But the challenges are worthwhile because creating in a virtual environment is truly an awesome experience and one of the most fun ways to use technology creatively.

## Project Details:

**Overview:** Students collaborate to design and create a virtual reality drawing based on a STEAM concept. Depending on the number of learners, the amount of equipment, and the STEAM content you want to cover, several approaches can be taken for this project. If you do not have the virtual reality system available, you can modify the project so students create a virtual gallery or slideshow instead of a live VR presentation.

**Timeline:** 2 to 6 hours

**Age/Skill Level:** This project is great for more advanced learners but can be scaled down and modified for any age and skill level by choosing simple STEAM concepts such as weather, geometry, animals, or seasons.

**Extended Version:** Once learners are comfortable with the concept of virtual reality, you may take the process one step further and do a live virtual reality drawing during a presentation. Record the creative process on video, showing both the virtual and real worlds, then share the video and pass along the learning.

## MATERIALS:

- 3D virtual drawing software with digital drawing input device (Google Tilt Brush, Gravity Sketch, CoolPaintrVR, Kingspray Graffiti, etc.)
- virtual reality viewer (Oculus, VIVE, etc.—and make sure the viewer is compatible with the other technology)
- computers, tablets, gaming device, or smartphones (dependent on the 3D software/device)
- paper and drawing supplies (optional)

**STEAM:** In this project, all the STEAM disciplines are equally represented.

**Instructions:**

1. To see what is possible and to inspire the learners, explore images and videos that show people drawing in virtual reality. Some are listed in the Resources section.

2. Invite learners to break into groups and choose the topic they will research and represent visually as a virtual drawing. Sample projects might be exploring geometry and engineering in the architecture of Ancient Greece, designing a deep space station, and so on.

3. Each group researches the topic collaboratively and organizes data and images for reference.

4. Design the virtual drawing, including what visual elements might be necessary and the colors and lines that might make the biggest impact.

5. Write the text of the presentation. This can be narrative or scientific, but there should be verbal cues for the visuals. The dialogue can be presented live or as prerecorded audio that is edited to match the visuals.

6. Practice the presentation in front of a small test audience and get feedback to make any necessary changes.

7. Share the final virtual reality drawing presentation.

8. Reflect on the process and post the results to share with others to pass on the learning.

Augmented and virtual reality are becoming major technologies, so check out timneedles.com for more project ideas, such as 3D portrait or object scanning, Pokémon Go Edu (I'm level 40), virtual history lessons, AR product design solutions, and VR field trips.

# PART III

# Next Level STEAM Learning

........................................................

**I**n this section we'll explore ways to strengthen the STEAM learning you are facilitating and elevate it to another level. Even the most experienced STEAM educators can continue growing their program by adding additional layers of engagement and activity. We'll begin with the most important element in expanding and deepening the work you are doing: connections.

# CHAPTER 12

## Connections

. . . . . . . . . . . . . . . . . . . .

**C**onnecting with others is one of the most powerful things we do in life; it unites us. Making connections is important for all educators, but it's essential for STEAM educators. By its nature, STEAM is collaborative, and connecting with others is necessary to stay updated on trends and developments. Great educators often have many strong connections; we as educators depend on one other and on our connections with people in our industry to keep our teaching relevant.

When you can connect STEAM learning with other disciplines, schools, and educational environments, it becomes more meaningful and memorable, but it doesn't need to stop there; reaching out to professionals can lead to lasting partnerships and directions for learning that we may have not envisioned. Many STEAM professionals from large companies, universities, and corporations make themselves available to educational groups and can give students a first-person perspective. You can make connections with these professionals through resources such as Commonwealth Scientific and Industrial Research Organisation (CSIRO), National Geographic Education's Explorer Classroom, and Hour of Code. Conferences, symposiums, and STEAM events are also great opportunities to connect. Professional social media accounts can be helpful; on LinkedIn, Twitter, and Instagram,

Making connections across disciplines allows learners to view any unit of study from different perspectives while uncovering its complexity and depth.

I have connected with fantastic people who ended up being great assets in my teaching.

While these connections are valuable for students, they can be even more so for educators because they can help us learn what new areas and technologies to pursue. STEAM is not a static curriculum, so effective STEAM teachers must follow innovations and adapt their curriculum with regularity, especially when it comes to addressing technology that is continuously developing.

## Sharing Success

Great learning is not enough to build a terrific STEAM program. Sharing that learning and its successes has become a necessity, and outreach also builds connections and creates opportunities you might not otherwise have. A strong STEAM program should communicate regularly with the school body or institution, the local community, and the worldwide STEAM community. The role of a teacher may start in the classroom, but it should spread through the community to be successful. If you take for granted that the wider audience understands why STEAM learning is important, you may miss an opportunity to build advocacy and understanding.

Great STEAM teachers need to share the positive things their students do in class, whether it's asking interesting questions, being a good collaborator, or even going back to the drawing board after a tough failure. Promote students for doing well but also for failing well, learning from their mistakes, and not getting down on themselves. Model the behavior and share your own successes and failures and how you learn from them. This modeling should be framed as a teachable moment so students can see what you were attempting, why you failed, how you learned something from reflecting on the failure, and most importantly, how you incorporated that learning and made a new attempt. This personal sharing builds trust and teaches an essential lesson on how to reflect and persevere.

New teachers might be apprehensive about personal sharing like this, but it can be beneficial and prepare you to face any fears you might have. Occasionally, students might see your failure as a weakness and challenge you on something you shared, especially if it is early in your relationship; a challenge such as this is often just a test, so react to it calmly and add context about the failures of well-known STEAM leaders and how they persevered. In other words, reframe the challenge.

## Social Media and Engaging Professionals

Social media is one of the easier ways to share and it has been a game changer for educators, especially in STEAM. It allows us to connect as colleagues and to share and learn from each other regularly. Sharing our work on social media extends the reach of the classroom to the world, and you never know who is going to see it. It helps to include the context about what was being learned and why it was important when sharing work to make a bigger impact. Connections made on social media can develop into meaningful relationships with professionals that continue to benefit students and educators for many years.

Many key individuals developing and using STEAM are also present online, so it's possible to connect with them and develop a greater awareness of the field. Major players accessible on Twitter, Instagram, Skype, and LinkedIn will occasionally connect with classes and play a role in projects. A project such as the STEAM trading cards (Chapter 6) can be shared on social media with the professionals portrayed on the cards, opening the door to communication with them. Sharing a project in this way can help it become more engaging and powerful and help inspire others.

Social media is constantly in flux, but that offers an opportunity for educators and learners because it is still very accessible. From an educator's point of view, this technology requires some planning because you need to consider your learners' responsibility level as you choose the way they'll communicate. And whether you have a class account, a teacher account, or your students are interacting on social media by themselves, review the media literacy guidelines before you get started.

## STEAM Career Exploration

An expanding variety of careers involve STEAM. Exploring trends in how the STEAM job market is evolving and diversifying can give both educators and learners a better idea of what to expect in the future.

Some occupations have obvious connections to STEAM, such as physicists, video game designers, and roboticists. The role of STEAM may be less obvious in others, such as fashion designers, ultrasound technicians, automotive engineers, or dietitians. For example, it might be clear how a dietitian would use math and science, but less obvious how they would interact with engineering, art, or technology. However, anyone who's been on a diet knows creativity is a major component of designing recipes and preparing food. This is an art form that continues to expand into the STEAM landscape with new trends such as molecular gastronomy, health apps, and assistive technology, and more accurate, multifaceted scales which make technology and engineering part of the new norm in the world of diets.

It's always a great project to research the ever-changing job market and the STEAM education requirements of different careers. Parents and colleagues who have or had jobs in the STEAM fields can be great resources. I've asked students to research careers and then team up to find local professionals in those careers, and it's led to some lasting connections. Students can share what they learn about STEAM careers with the school, organization, administration, and community to educate them and also to advocate for STEAM education.

**PROFESSIONAL PERSPECTIVE**
Melodie Yashar

There's still a perceptual divide between technical knowledge or "know-how" and skill sets that are traditionally known as "creative" ones. I encounter that even now in the work that I do within NASA Ames Human-Computer Interaction and in academia too. It's challenging because you almost have to be a little bit of both in order to foster the conversations and do the inter-disciplinary work that's actually meaningful and transgressive and that gets the attention of subject matter experts in each discipline.

# Virtual and Real-World Field Trips

Field trips to see how STEAM works in the real world can be amazing learning experiences for everyone involved. The trips, which can be done in person or virtually, can inspire project ideas, give educators and learners ideas about areas to explore, and introduce emerging technologies that might be interesting to use in class.

In-person field trips generally make a bigger impact and can develop from the kinds of connections we discussed in the previous section. If it's too difficult or costly to take students on a field trip, a great alternative is to bring local STEAM professionals into class. This kind of interaction can take a bit of organization, so it often makes sense to widen the scope. You can invite a few STEAM professionals to talk in a larger discussion to make the experience more of an event.

If in-person visits aren't possible, video conferencing technology allows for interaction to happen virtually, regardless of the classroom's location in the world. The technology is free and accessible as well as adaptable to nearly any circumstance. Remember, nothing brings home the point more than seeing some amazing STEAM work happening in action.

# Working with Professional Makerspaces, Maker Fairs, and Museums

Professional makerspaces and other STEAM work centers are becoming more numerous in communities around the world, and they often have outreach programs for schools and the community. Bigger cities usually have multiple makerspaces and STEAM labs; these might have different focuses, so some research might be required. This is another area where connections come in handy, so be sure to check with other educators and professionals before researching from scratch.

Maker or STEAM fairs are another way to find connections, resources, and information. There are major name-brand fairs for makers as well as local grassroots fairs; both are great for finding new collaborators and learning new technologies, and they can showcase the work you're doing in the classroom with students. You can also create your own maker fair to develop a program closer to home that benefits the community.

National and local museums often have programs that cater to education and teachers. In addition to facilitating connections, many have educational programs that familiarize teachers and students with all they have to offer. I have found great books, videos, and items that have aided my teaching, plus a plethora of online resources such as 3D scans of objects,

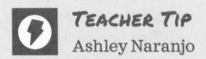

### TEACHER TIP
Ashley Naranjo

As more museums provide access to their digitized collections and offer opportunities for online chats with historians, scientists, and other experts, classrooms are now connected to more resources than ever before that can serve as the building blocks for these authentic learning experiences.

VR field trips, and scanned original documents that have added authenticity and engagement to our learning.

## Conventions, Conferences, and Symposiums

Professional organizations offer conventions for every subject taught, but I find the best conferences mix different subjects and focus on bigger issues. ISTE hosts several gatherings, including the Creative Constructor Lab, and its annual national conference is an amazing place to connect to like-minded educators. Groups such as the Association for Supervision and Curriculum Development (ASCD), Future of Education Technology Conference (FETC), and CUE also run focused conventions as well as large national conferences.

Smaller conferences have their place too. Those that focus on STEAM might offer fewer connections than the big events, but those highly specialized contacts may be even more helpful. Regional gatherings are important for educators who have financial or geographic limitations. Even unconferences and college symposiums can be great places to get and share information and make lasting connections.

Technology is an ally for educators with limitations because even if you can't attend a conference, you can follow those who do through hashtags on social media. Another increasingly available option is virtual attendance at conferences; technology-aware associations such as ISTE now allow participants to watch presentations and interact from home.

## Navigating the World of Educational Technology

Trying to figure out which educational technology works best for you and your learners can be overwhelming. The world of technology moves quickly, and new tools come out all the time. Keeping up can be stressful, especially for new teachers or educators who don't regularly integrate technology. Educators don't want to miss out on anything that could be beneficial to their students, but they might have a hard time knowing which tools are valuable.

Here's my advice: organize your search, find trustworthy colleagues who regularly share valuable tools, and work with your professional learning network. You're not searching alone; many other teachers are sorting through the same technology you are, so working together is beneficial. It may not always be clear whether a tool is beneficial if you don't know how to apply it, so it's valuable to hear how colleagues are using the tool. I find the majority of my new technology tools through conferences, maker events, and social media, but I come across so much technology that I might not recall it later, and I've learned to keep notes with pictures. These notes are essential for me because they allow me to revisit the tools when I have more time to learn about them, or when I'm searching for a tool to use in a lesson.

The benefit of conferences and events is that you can often have a hands-on experience with the technology. That gives you greater insight into how it works and might function in your teaching. The strength of social media posts from other educators is that they may have used it in the classroom, and they may include lesson or project ideas. Be aware that some educators posting edtech are not sharing for the sake of sharing; some are paid by companies to be influencers or are supported in other ways that are not immediately clear. This is not to say you shouldn't be open to what they're sharing, but it's something to consider in your decision making. This is one of the reasons I suggest having multiple sources for your edtech tool contacts on social media; collecting more perspectives tends to offer more solid leads.

Tools that are right for one educator, however, may not serve the needs of another. Experiment to see which tools are right for you. I avoid certain technology tools because of privacy issues; others may be too costly or difficult to integrate into the computers and lab I have. Decide what works for you. I think of educational technology the way I think of music: just because something is at the top of the chart doesn't mean I'm going to like it, and conversely, I may love something that's not charting at all. You never know.

# Online Connections

When you connect online with other people, it's important to be clear and courteous. Context is crucial in what you're communicating, and when something is implied but not specifically stated, misunderstandings can occur. Different generations and cultures have different norms and expectations. Younger learners, for example, may use some abbreviations and vocabulary that can be confusing to older people. When my parents bought smartphones and we began texting, they didn't understand memes or common phrases such as "LOL," so I had to explain them. Be conscious of the language you use in online interactions and lean toward clarity. The most common online miscommunication often occurs with humor, sarcasm, and idiomatic phrases, because those don't always translate to other places or cultures. Start slowly and make conversation before diving in too deep. In online communications, there is a tendency to cut to the chase, but it can come off rude or overly assertive.

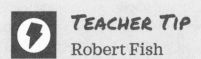

## TEACHER TIP
### Robert Fish

. . . . . . . . . . . . . . . . . . . . . . . . . . . . . . . . . . . . . . . . . . . . . .

When you put people together for a conversation online, it's just like it is in person: you have to start with some normal social interactions to break down barriers and get people comfortable with one another. You can't just jump into deep questions. Once you let people get to know each other, even superficially, it allows you to get to deeper interactions.

# Preparing for an Unknown Future

We cannot predict the future. Educators can use the past and the present to project what to expect for students, but it's not a perfect science. If we base our assumptions on the increasing speed of technological change and continued automation, we can forecast that future careers will be vastly different from those of today. So how do you prepare students for an unknown future? How do you navigate educating students for future occupations for which we likely don't yet have names? Do we try to make our best guess?

If we do, we will likely be wrong. Look at the past: there are a handful of surprisingly accurate predictions, but most depictions of what the future would be like are wildly inaccurate. A wiser approach is to build skills that we know are useful, such as those outlined in the ISTE Standards, update our information regularly, and strengthen students' abilities to be creative, flexible, and innovative. This approach pairs naturally with STEAM learning and works in tandem with it. It's important to occasionally step back and examine the curriculum to be sure this is all being reflected in the projects and assignments. Teachers often lean toward one discipline or another and sometimes grow too comfortable in what they teach, but it's vital to make sure students are getting a well-balanced, modern STEAM experience.

When I was in middle school in the 1980s, my teachers predicted computers were going to be the key tool of the future. They were correct. But the way they chose to prepare us to work in this new computer-centered world was with keyboarding classes. In retrospect, it was not the best skill set to build, but I understand why they chose it. At the time, keyboards were the new technology, replacing punch cards and other computer input methods, but being an amazing typist today doesn't give anyone a huge edge in the digital world. In truth, keyboards themselves now seem antiquated as devices evolve, touchpads grow more dominant, and voice controls become more ubiquitous. I can envision keyboards disappearing in the next ten years.

I don't fault my teachers for not preparing me fully for the digital age. As an educator, I understand how easy it is to base your teaching on present circumstances. Knowing how quickly technology moves, I can't even guess where it is going, but I can foresee some of the necessary skills. Many of the most essential skills are reflected in the ISTE Student Standards and the Framework for 21st Century Learning. In addition to those skills, educators must help students learn the power of adaptability because it will likely be a requisite of any future occupation.

## Jobs Without Titles

In education, there has been an ongoing discussion about how to prepare students for jobs in an unpredictable future, but the scenario also applies to education itself. The world is becoming more automated, and it has affected nearly every occupation. I think we can see this trend continuing, but we also must consider what other consequences come with it. Social and emotional learning becomes a factor here because it is not enough to simply prepare students for STEAM careers; educators should also help those students develop the skills and ability to adapt and persevere so they can exist happily and successfully in those careers.

When I began working as a teacher more than twenty years ago, the job appeared predictable and secure; teachers learned the curriculum and taught it their whole career. But that approach doesn't work today. Shortly after I started teaching, the duties and expectations of a teacher began evolving and changing. I helped introduce more computers into my school, and they quickly replaced all the analog equipment. I was able to learn and adapt in part because I worked with students as partners in experimenting and innovating with the new tools. Many of those students I worked with benefited from our partnership, went on to become masters of those emerging tools, and now have amazing professional careers. I make it a point to continue our communication in part because of the bonds we built, but also to keep the learning with my current students relevant.

Alumni can be an amazing resource, and social media allows for a direct connection. These relationships help inform students about potential occupations and industry trends and expectations. Fostering communication between alumni and current students has had numerous benefits, some of which were unexpected. It is terrific to be able to celebrate the hard work and success of former students, but the interaction also helps current students understand the value of a strong work ethic and the unpredictable nature of the job market. We discuss not only the successes but also the failures as they sometimes teach a more impactful lesson.

# CHAPTER 13

# Collaboration

. . . . . . . . . . . . . . . . . . . . . . .

Collaboration is an essential digital age skill that can bring STEAM learning to another level for both students and educators. Some people have a natural ability to work with others, while some will need practice. Either way, working together is an essential component of STEAM work that learners and educators must master to be successful. Whether your students are working with each other or you're working with colleagues, there can be obstacles involved in collaborations. But it's important to view them as challenges instead of roadblocks. Every situation is different and comes with unique opportunities and expectations. The key to successful collaboration is trust and good communication—they're necessities in working together well. Checking in with each other as you are working together will alleviate many of the issues that may arise.

Although the biggest issue in collaborative work is often miscommunication and false assumptions, there are times when personality issues can get in the way. A few factors can sour a productive collaboration, the biggest being ego. The best way to overcome that is to have a common goal focused on learning and results. But even a difficult collaboration can be rewarding and teach a great deal. Navigating the partnership will be easier if you are aware of the kind of person you are and what you are comfortable with. Avoid bringing judgment into the equation; when issues arise, it is better to work on solving them than laying blame. Afterward, you can reflect and assess what may have led to the issues, then revise the process.

Collaboration benefits learners of every age. The dynamic between students will be a factor in any learning situation because they will have their own social concerns and skill sets that will be important to manage. I always try to tailor the collaboration to the group of learners I'm working with because every group has different strengths and weaknesses that need to be considered. My biggest priority is to make sure there is balance and that everyone plays a role in the project. To help in this effort, I find it helpful to have students document their roles and the work each person does in the process.

## Types of Collaborations

Before you begin collaborating, consider your timeline and how much time students will have for interaction so that you can choose the best model to organize and structure the work. There are a variety of ways to incorporate collaboration, from having students work together in class, to partnering with other classes in school, to virtual and global collaboration. I will outline the different types of collaborations, but it is always important to consider how you structure the work and interactions themselves.

- Collaborating Within the District or Organization

  The best place to look for people to work with is generally within your home district or organization. Collaborating with colleagues within your school or organization allows for regular contact and face-to-face communication. One obvious benefit is that you often share the same students. The culture of the school or organization may facilitate and support collaboration or hamper it, so that might affect how you proceed. Working together with direct colleagues can build bonds, and the learning can extend and stay productive for many years, for both students and educators.

- Local and National Collaborations

  Working with neighboring schools or community groups can lead to lasting partnerships and connections. Schools or groups that are out of the area in different states, provinces, and so on, can increase learning and social engagement and teach students about the different ways people live. Pairing with both local and long-distance schools can be especially interesting.

- Global Collaborations

  Collaborating with learners in other countries can be a fantastic experience because it adds layers of additional learning about culture and history and always makes for a memorable experience. These kinds of partnerships can build bridges that last and offer students insight into different perspectives as well as various cultural priorities and approaches to STEAM.

# First-Time Collaborations

If you are new to collaborating, it helps to build slowly and not put too much pressure on yourself or your students. As with technology, I find it helps to do some beta testing. When I am going to engage in a collaboration project, I often do a short test run with a small group of engaged, excited students. I work with them closely to iron out any issues that might occur so that those are solved before I engage the full group of students. Not every project allows time for this, but it's helpful if you can manage it because the feedback from the students often inspires changes that you can incorporate into the class collaboration.

If you are just starting, don't raise the expectations too high, because it can ruin the experience if you don't meet them. Working together, especially with learners from other places, is important learning itself so begin modestly and adjust the process as you continue the work. I have also found that inviting other educators and students from outside of my classes has been beneficial because their experiences and reflections can add another perspective. Embrace the unexpected when you collaborate, and be open to what comes your way. You'll often be surprised, and sometimes it leads to magical moments with lasting impact.

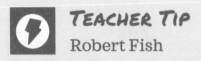

### TEACHER TIP
Robert Fish

· · · · · · · · · · · · · · · · · · · · · · · · · · · · · · · · · · · · · · · · · · · · · · · · · · · · · · · · ·

For a first collaboration, you want to keep it simple, you want to try to work with technologies that you're already comfortable with, or that someone you are working with is comfortable with. Keep the first collaboration short so that it's low stakes.

# Collaboration Advice

Regardless of what type of collaboration you engage in, there are a few elements that make any partnership easier and more successful. Here are a few that work in every situation:

- Educational Priorities and Expectations

  *What do you want students to learn? What results do you expect?*

  Set clear educational priorities and expectations and communicate those with your partners. This is vital because different groups from various parts of the world often have different expectations and may assume the same from their partner. It helps to understand what basic learning and results you hope the collaboration will yield and communicate that with any partners.

- Communication, Schedule, and Limitations

  *How will learners collaborate and communicate? What scheduling or privacy issues are there?*

  This is a vital step that can make or break a collaborative project. Setting a schedule for projects, with regular opportunities for collaboration and communication, is essential. Depending on where your partners are in the world, this can be a big roadblock if you plan on live interactions using video or audio. Different countries have different privacy and security measures when it comes to students, so using their names or showing their faces may be against the rules unless you're communicating using a totally closed system. Even if you're in the same time zone, it's still necessary to pay attention to these issues, because you don't want to waste time that can be used for learning waiting for the other group to respond or add input. Interaction keeps learners engaged, so if you plan a timeline with regular interactions, the project will be more successful.

• Clear, Itemized Tasks and Responsibilities

*What are students in each group expected to do and when should it be done?*

When collaborating with other groups, it's best to clearly communicate each step. Break down what learners are expected to do and when they should do it so things move along at the right pace for all involved. This includes even simple elements such as formalizing introductions, getting to know your activities, and creating a timeline for them.

• Summative Reflection

*What did we learn? What additional or unexpected learning occurred?*

It's always helpful for teachers and students to reflect at the end of a lesson or project, but it may be even more important with collaborations because so much unexpected learning tends to occur. Point out precisely what was learned and why it's important in terms of the STEAM content and any additional cultural or social learning. Small moments of surprise learning can be teachable and memorable when shared with the full group of learners. This reflection is also valuable for teachers because we can grow from each experience, incorporate what works into other projects, and remove or alter what doesn't.

## Connecting with Collaboration Partners

Many organizations can facilitate collaborative exchanges, including iEARN, Global Nomads, the Japan Society, and National Geographic Education and additional online resources on my website. Some of these organizations are formal and require applications and online meetings or classes before the program, while others facilitate partnerships and leave the rest up to you. Consider your needs and time allowance before choosing a group. You can also make your own connections through social media or at international conferences such as the ISTE Conference & Expo.

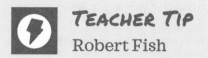

## TEACHER TIP
### Robert Fish

One of the biggest challenges is finding collaborators to work with, but I found there are often multiple people in your school or community who might have connections with potential collaborators. It's not a bad way to get started—especially if it's an international collaboration—because you have some cultural knowledge and you know the person on the other end of the interaction, so it's a little easier to work through difficulties.

# Doing Projects for Your Community and the World

Some of the most powerful STEAM lessons are those that connect to the community. Consider what problems exist in your community that may have solutions based in STEAM. It's also helpful to connect with community organizations, both for resources and potential collaborations. If you extend this philosophy one step further, you can make the collaboration global. This can be even more powerful, whether it's partnering with a foreign community for collaboration or doing charitable STEAM lessons that benefit people in other countries.

# Creating with Professionals and Local STEAM Industries

Wherever you are in the world, there are likely professionals nearby who may offer assistance and give students an authentic glimpse into real-world STEAM. There are a variety of approaches to introducing this into a learning environment, from having a guest speaker to collaborating with a local industry that incorporates STEAM. There are many opportunities available online as well; some of my favorites are listed in the Resources.

Start by looking at alumni or local businesses that incorporate elements of STEAM. Alumni are especially powerful because they were in the same seat as students, and they show students it's possible to succeed in STEAM industries.

It's important to frame this kind of collaboration with learners so they can make the most of the opportunity and have good questions to ask in the moment. There are also a few precautions to be aware of when communicating with people who are not familiar with the classroom setting, because they may not be aware of the impact their words and ideas might have on learners, especially younger learners. Context is key in these types of situations, so if guests are sharing their stories, it's important to note that what may be true for one person is not necessarily true for everyone. This becomes especially important if guests start sharing opinions rather than facts. For example, if a guest says they don't think college is necessary, you may want to reframe that and note that while it may not have been necessary for your guest, it certainly helps and is expected elsewhere in the industry.

## Working with Other Disciplines

The concept of STEAM encompasses science, technology, engineering, art, and math, but it doesn't need to be limited to those five subjects. It can be productive to bring in additional disciplines and subjects along with STEAM. Whether it's pairing with a history class to make laser-cut recreations of landmarks or working with a business class to create a business plan for a STEAM company, these collaborations can add dimension to lessons. An added benefit to this kind of work is that it brings together different ideas and perspectives, which can strengthen and diversify the learning.

**PROFESSIONAL PERSPECTIVE**
Melodie Yashar

I think there's always a danger in becoming highly specialized, siloed, and not thinking about large nasty problems in a holistic way or in a way that draws from other knowledge or that grows and evolves in more integrated and holistic ways.

## Collaboration and Technology

When you collaborate over a longer distance, you'll need to incorporate technology such as social media or audio/video conferences to make the partnership work. This technology can be a terrific way to connect, but it also can cause issues and frustrations. Here are some important things to consider when choosing which technology to use and how to use it.

First, consider the needs and constraints of both partners in the collaboration. What technology do they have that's accessible? What privacy concerns might there be? What times are they available? What digital safety concerns might each partner have? These questions become more important when the collaboration is international or with a business or institution, as they will often have different concerns. In my personal and professional experience, I have used nearly every piece of collaboration technology out there, and the best collaborations tend to allow face-to-face interactions through video conferencing. This is not always possible, and you may have to resort to another method, but there are many video conferencing programs available these days that work well in the classroom, often with support for education, including **Skype, Google Classroom, Adobe Connect, Zoom, Microsoft Teams, ClickMeeting, Cisco Webex, BlueJeans Meetings, Join.me**, and **GoToMeeting**, to name a few. I've also worked with groups such as iEARN, the Japan Society, and the Global Nomads, as well as professional associations such as ISTE and National Art Education Association (NAEA), which have created collaboration portals that are streamlined for educators.

Always have a backup plan because sometimes the technology fails. You don't want to have to improvise with impatient students if the connections aren't working on the devices or the Wi-Fi gives out. It helps to plan and have an alternate activity in case there are technical errors, because even when things are double-checked and everything is planned out, errors sometimes occur.

The most important consideration is whether the technology is truly serving the project. Video conferencing or collaboration technology should never impede the learning, only enhance it, so if you find it causing too many issues, you may need to reconsider your choices and find a method of collaborating that works better for your situation.

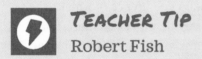

## Teacher Tip
Robert Fish

Make sure that the technology is a tool, or at the very least a support, and don't allow the technology to get in the way when collaborating. It shouldn't be about the technology. At some point when you're doing this kind of interaction, it should be completely obvious to the kids why having this interaction is central to whatever it is they're trying to be doing without you having to explain it to them, so they're not like, "Well, this is fun but why am I doing it?"

# CHAPTER 14

# Authenticity

. . . . . . . . . . . . . . . . . . . . .

One of the secrets to great, impactful STEAM lessons is a simple concept—keep it real. Authenticity is a term you often hear discussed in educational circles, but it doesn't necessarily mean the same thing to everyone. When I talk about authenticity, I really mean two elements: The first is the learning and projects, and the second is the teaching. Authentic learning means that student work reflects the real world. Whenever possible, the lessons and projects occurring in schools should mirror what's occurring professionally. When you can merge the interests of the students with the authentic work happening in STEAM careers, it will lead to more transformative learning.

When I was in school, I often had the feeling that some of the projects we were doing were pointless. Math teachers frequently seem to get asked why people should learn their subject, and it can be challenging to explain why math is important, aside from finances. When in doubt, turn back toward STEAM, because math is at the core of how most technology works. It's not enough for STEAM projects and learning to be relevant; educators also need to communicate why the learning will help their students succeed. I'd go a step further and suggest that after projects conclude, students reflect on their learning to make sure they understand both what they learned and why it was important.

The second aspect of authenticity is about the teaching and how it appears to students. All educators have different styles of teaching, but students can also tell if you are engaged and excited by what you're teaching. If you really care, it can be contagious. Honesty has a way of cutting through the words we speak and potentially turning on disengaged learners, so it can change the climate of the classroom or learning space.

## Future Ready Teaching

We've learned that part of our job as educators is also keeping an eye on the future and helping students prepare for careers that will emerge and be vital in the STEAM world. The positive aspect of this issue is that, as educators we do not need to do all the work ourselves: thanks to the internet and social media, the education community is now connected, so we can share and pool our resources. Having a great professional learning network, or PLN, is important when teaching STEAM because we deal with emerging technologies and topics that evolve quickly. Great educators today need to be connected and collaborative or they risk falling behind and teaching outdated material.

The unfortunate truth is that there are teachers who are not on board with this vision, and it may be because they are not connected, or they are not happy in their own lives, or they might be in the wrong profession. In more than two decades of teaching, I've seen a few people who probably shouldn't be teaching, and I found they can negatively impact others. If you are to succeed as an educator, you want to enjoy what you are doing and feel good about helping learners find their way. I advise you to avoid that kind of negativity because it can bring you down and squash your enthusiasm.

## Big Questions

Addressing real issues allows for experiences with deeper meaning and authenticity, but these types of problems may not have tidy answers and results. This can frustrate and deter some students. The key things to remember are that we need to focus on the learning and that we are preparing learners for situations they will potentially deal with in the adult world.

There is also a value in posing and addressing some of these questions about real-world issues because it brings an awareness of a topic and its realities. You never know the impact you may have on students; the topic may inspire someone to go into that field and help discover a solution later in life. A project such as this can also help both educators and learners engage more deeply, which can lead to more beneficial results while also teaching the material. Whether you choose to focus on redesigning your school court-yard to make it more accessible to students or you take on the global energy crisis using real issues that affect students, it makes STEAM learning more authentic, even if you don't always find a solution.

Focus on the learning and frame issues that arise as teachable moments. Bringing school or local community problems into the classroom and searching for STEAM-based solutions requires an educator to be in the moment and aware of how students are learning from the process and how they are feeling. Most learners (and teachers, for that matter) are not accustomed to dealing with a lesson that might not come to a clear conclusion, so it may be necessary to end the project without a solution and reflect on the learning alone. This is an important real-world lesson, even if there is no clear conclusion.

This is a good place to revisit our STEAM mindset and remind students that frustration, failure, and confusion are often part of the process. Tackling real-world problems will teach everyone, including the educators, expected and possibly unexpected lessons, so it helps to communicate the learning through a journal or some type of reflective media such as a blog or wiki. The approaches to the issues themselves are valuable even if they don't lead to solutions, so remember to focus on the learning and to look for teachable moments.

# Reflecting Professional Atmospheres in the Classroom

I always enjoy researching real-world STEAM environments and then adapting our learning environment to include as many aspects of them as possible. This can be done as a STEAM design project itself, and because it affects the students so directly, it helps create a positive atmosphere of respect and collaboration in school.

# Approaching Real-World Questions and STEAM Problems

We touched on the topic of bringing real-world issues into the learning environment earlier, but let's look at it in more detail and examine some of the positives and negatives for learners and educators. Whenever possible, let your STEAM lessons focus on real questions that affect the lives of students, such as energy, housing, and the environment.

Lessons like these can open students' eyes to the fact that they can change the world around them. There are, however, some potential issues to be aware of when exploring real-world issues in the learning environment. One of them is that these lessons may trigger some students who have encountered these issues in a personal way. A real-world problem may bring a new reality to the learning environment, and other students might not know how to react and be supportive.

This is where social and emotional learning comes back into play. Knowing how to support students who may be triggered is an important thing to know beforehand. It's human nature to want to console someone who is emotionally distraught, but it's important not to try to quiet them or stop them from crying. The feelings coming out are okay, and it helps to let them know that and give them space to express those feelings. Everyone is different, so there are no right answers for how to deal with some of these kinds of issues, but an educator's reaction is usually a model for their students, and they'll often follow your example.

# Everyday STEAM

A great way to approach authentic learning is by using the everyday world around us and finding the connections to STEAM. Whether it's examining local community issues or everyday household problems, finding a STEAM connection adds a relatable and memorable aspect to the learning. Finding the connections can be tricky, but the answers are often in plain sight. You may have to change your perspective to see them. As an artist, I can instinctively find connections to art and design, but when I look for a connection to science, I often find it naturally involves math, technology, and engineering.

As an example, I teach in a school not far from the beach, so some natural topics for us are wind farms that are being proposed off the coast or how the Army Corps of Engineers is attempting to design jetties to stop erosion. Both of these ideas implement all the areas of STEAM in projects the students can see unfold. Localized learning topics can allow for more connections because projects are based in the community, and there is often outreach available from local programs. Every community faces different challenges, so it's a terrific place to begin looking for authentic STEAM connections.

Another way to find daily STEAM connections is by looking at daily problems and issues that arise. Whenever I'm faced with a problem in daily life—whether it's losing my ID card or finding more comfortable, durable shoes—I make a note of it to see how it might be solved using STEAM. These daily issues may seem minor, but they can often lead the way to an interesting STEAM challenge. Elements such as fashion, school, housing, transportation, and entertainment are loaded with possibilities for STEAM connections for learning.

Consider the audience and their perspective when looking for authentic ways to connect STEAM to learners. What things do your learners interact with daily and care about most? Finding the connections from those to STEAM can be powerful. Some areas are easier than others, but the connections are often there if you explore and dive deep. For example, many students are interested in film and television. This is a great STEAM topic itself, but if you investigate some of their favorite movies and television shows, you can find tons of fascinating connections there as well, ranging from creating Iron Man's suit in the *Avengers* movies to the technology behind filming *Stranger Things* to the biology of SpongeBob SquarePants.

The last approach I'll mention is one of my favorites: Turn the search for everyday STEAM over to the students themselves. If you ask learners to be mindful of what they do every day and keep a lookout for the connections to STEAM, they always return with some unexpected and interesting results. You may have to model this challenge and share some of your findings to help them see how to be open and view things from another perspective, but they are more likely to remember their own findings than anything you present. This can be a great lesson, because in addition to finding STEAM connections in their life, it requires learners to be more present in the moment—a positive social and emotional learning life lesson as well.

# CHAPTER 15

# Sustainability

. . . . . . . . . . . . . . . . . . . . . . . .

**A**s STEAM educators, we deal with some unique challenges due to rapid technology development and the need to stay up-to-date. We need to watch how technology is developing and make sure we're bringing any important new tools or trends into the classroom. We also need to incorporate material that addresses real-world challenges such as caring for the environment, preserving natural resources, and dealing with local community issues that can range from sustainable housing to recycling. In addition to thinking sustainably when approaching curriculum and technology, we also need to consider sustainable approaches for our well-being. In this chapter, I'll explore sustainability in education as well as in social and emotional learning for teachers and students.

## STEAM Project Variety

Keeping STEAM projects varied and dynamic is important in maintaining students' interest levels. It's helpful to change things up at regular intervals and use different technologies to keep a fresh perspective and maintain student engagement while also giving them time to absorb and digest the material. Early on, consider the skill sets you want students to have when they complete the course and break the skills down so the students can learn them over time. I vary the difficulty level and technology used by students to match their abilities because it alleviates potential student frustration.

## Student Choice

Working with students as collaborators can be powerful and sustainable in terms of learning. When you offer students options and open up the class with student choice, the learning becomes more impactful for both the teacher and the students. Some educators can have a hard time giving up that sense of power and control at first, but collaboration is where real digital age learning begins. Giving students choice can also be a bit difficult to navigate early on, especially if students aren't used to having a voice in their learning.

One of the most popular ways to implement student choice is borrowed from the technology industry: Google allows its employees to spend 20% of their time working autonomously on a passion project that will benefit the company, and a variant of this concept of "20% time" has been popularized in schools as "magic hour" or "genius hour." The time frame is dependent on the educator and the students, but the basic principle behind all these ideas is the same: allow students to choose their own projects, which are generally collaborative. Students need to show learning, share what they learned and what they contributed to the project, and demonstrate how the work fulfills a set of STEAM requirements. These projects can be implemented in various time frames, from an hour a week, to a large summative choice project that incorporates various skills, to full choice-based classes in which students direct themselves. When you begin implementing choice, it's important to help learners keep a sense of structure and take responsibility for sharing and reflecting on their process and results. Letting the learners be autonomous gives them a sense of direction over their learning and empowers them to follow their curiosities.

# Learner Autonomy

The natural extension of student choice is learner autonomy. This grants the students not only decision-making power but also responsibility, which is important because it reflects the real-world scenarios learners will experience in life. Some students may be ready for it before others, so depending on grade level, age, maturity level, skills of the learner, it can be personalized. When the concept of autonomy is introduced, many learners have difficulty at first, especially if they've been conditioned in a traditional industrial-age school system. For that reason, it's helpful to move in the direction of autonomy slowly, by first introducing elements of choice and projects such as genius or magic hour.

Whether you are moving toward autonomy or taking it on completely, it is beneficial for students to own and direct their education and learn personal responsibility for their choices and learning. I don't want to be one of those "in my day" teachers, but I'm sure many others can relate to the shock of entering college and suddenly having to learn personal accountability because high school had been so structured. The approach that existed in school systems such as the one I attended made students dependent on teachers, and we didn't gain the essential skill of learning how to teach ourselves and embrace the idea of being a lifelong learner. In today's world, there are vast resources available for learners to aid themselves in their independent learning, and as educators, we can act more as guides.

# Diversifying STEAM Technology

Technology moves quickly, and what's emerging today may be gone tomorrow, so it's necessary to always incorporate a variety of technology. Use a few different technological options (apps, programs, tools, and so on) when teaching students. Because technology and STEAM learning develop so fast, I make it a point to experiment and add at least one new piece of technology each semester. Always remember to teach process and ideas, not simply technology. The technology will likely change in the future, but the process and learning can remain.

# STEAM Equity and Access

Creating an equitable STEAM curriculum is a factor that educators should consider when designing their curriculum. Learners should have access regardless of gender, income, race, geography, sexuality, or any other factor. Historically, there has been an imbalance in STEM; adding art into the mix is helpful, but some of the bias that may exist in education might not be obvious. Project choices, availability, costs involved, or even the attitudes of parents and students can all be factors that may cause an imbalance, so it's necessary for educators to actively promote equity.

Organizations and programs such as NASA, Girls Who Code, the National Science Foundation, NACME, and National Girls Collaborative Project have worked to try to add balance by actively recruiting different groups of people into STEM and STEAM. They have made some progress, but it's a factor every educator should think about. Adding diverse projects, student choice, student voice, and social justice into education helps create a well-balanced learning environment. The key is not taking equity for

## PROFESSIONAL PERSPECTIVE
Melodie Yashar

I really do believe that it starts as early as elementary school—this perception that science, technology, and engineering are "too difficult" or "too challenging." I believe this (false) perception prevents young women and others from following that academic path. In my opinion, there's hardly a sense that as a young woman in a technical or scientific field that you're in a supportive environment to fail or falter and learn from the experience. That was my experience—there was an element of anxiety that I wasn't going to have a support system in place. If I completely bombed something like an exam, I would have wanted to know that I could simply recover from it and demonstrate resilience to just move on and not beat myself up about it. I never really had a support system in place to tell me that.

granted as a teacher or administrator. Implementing STEAM curriculum that appeals to all learners has benefits beyond equity because it helps build the program and adds new perspectives to the learning as well.

## Social and Emotional Learning

In education, social and emotional learning (SEL) and other mindfulness programs have become popular. They may include a variety of different approaches and elements, including everything from meditation and yoga to anti-bullying campaigns and community outreach. The programs can differ, but the core concept behind social and emotional learning is that we as educators should consider the emotional as well as academic needs of our students. This also extends to ourselves as educators and the other professionals around us.

There are productive ways to pair STEAM and SEL in lessons. One of the most valuable ways of incorporating mindfulness is working it directly into the curriculum; there is a lot of interesting research that can provide a foundation for a STEAM lesson on mindfulness. There are also elements of art therapy, movement, and new technology that can support mindful learning as well.

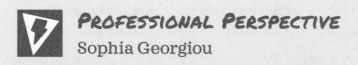

### PROFESSIONAL PERSPECTIVE
Sophia Georgiou

•  •  •  •  •  •  •  •  •  •  •  •  •  •  •  •  •  •  •  •  •  •  •  •  •  •  •  •  •  •  •

Everyone is an individual, and each person will approach the world differently. I think teachers can help their students by listening to them, seeing what they excel at and enjoy, and inspiring them to want to learn more. Learning is constant and evolving.

### Student Mindfulness

There are different ways to work social and emotional learning into a STEAM lesson, and the depth and extent of the lesson will depend on the audience and the environment. This kind of learning can be included in short bursts over time or as full projects, but I'd suggest focusing on moments when we know students can be stressed, such as early in the school year, before big exams, before vacations, and after personal, school, or community incidents.

Using technology that addresses mindfulness might be the easiest approach to begin with because it generally also touches on science, math, and art. Several mindfulness and meditation apps such as **Calm**, **Headspace**, **Buddhify**, and **Aura** can be used as a foundation, and I have found great success teaching students elements of mindfulness by starting this way.

## Teacher Mindfulness

To keep our STEAM teaching sustainable, we also need to take care of ourselves. Be in the moment and check in with yourself as a teacher. This is especially necessary at points during the year when we tend to be stressed or worn out. Our emotions as educators can often mirror those of our students; a great example is feeling both excited and anxious as school begins each year. Even after teaching for more than twenty years, this is still true for me. It's useful to understand that students are often in the same mental state.

Good class planning can alleviate many problems and help us avoid over-working or overextending ourselves. The antiquated idea that a teacher can stick to the same old curriculum without adapting isn't the reality of STEAM educators because the field is constantly evolving. But introducing too many new elements too soon can be overwhelming. To avoid burnout, alternate between difficult and easy material to teach so that you can follow up a section that's hard to teach with elements that you're comfortable with.

It's also beneficial when educators model their mindfulness practices and social and emotional learning for their students. This is one of the areas where it really does help to practice what you preach. Sharing your positive coping tools as well as your shortcomings is important because no one is perfect, and failure is always full of teachable moments. When sharing is authentic, it can give learners a better sense of the realities of managing stress or emotions and making decisions. This is often a work in progress, and not a lesson we learn once and apply forever.

I try to begin the STEAM learning with a fun, short, and easy project, an amuse-bouche of what is to come to start the process off on a positive note. Planning it, I know it's necessary to design a project in which everyone can succeed, and I also incorporate the student's names and faces in the project so I can get to know them better. The fact that I start the class with a hands-on project gives students a better impression of what to expect, but it's also helpful if the learning is fun and meaningful.

## Decision Fatigue

Being an educator means making an enormous number of decisions daily. This can often lead to decision fatigue, so it's important to be mindful of when this happens and give yourself some quiet time to refresh. I find I occasionally need to "zone out" after teaching, so I'll make art, listen to music or comedy, exercise, have a healthy snack, or sometimes just stare out into space quietly to rejuvenate myself. The biggest problem with decision fatigue is that after we hit our tipping point making decisions, we often are incapable of deciding anything—or worse, more apt to make bad decisions. This problem is especially relevant to us as STEAM educators because we are often in uncharted waters as we experiment with fast-moving tech-nologies, deal with unexpected issues that arise, and lead students into areas where we don't know all the answers. In a sense, we are the decisions we make in life, so choosing to be more mindful of our stress levels and emotional health needs to be a priority if we are to be successful.

We also need to remember that students often suffer from decision fatigue as much as educators. This is why we all need to embrace these social and

Here's an example of a collaborative project that includes much of the next level STEAM learning discussed in this section. it began with a mural and thanks to the connections with colleagues and National Geographic, along with students authentic interests, it evolved to incorporate a series of sustainable, continuing projects.

emotional learning skills to cope and to take care of ourselves and be aware of our emotional state. Decision fatigue can become a greater issue for students when they have more choice or educational autonomy because they are making more decisions on their own. It doesn't mean it's not worth reaching for that choice and autonomy, but it does require us to be positive role models and tell our students when we see them unable to make good decisions.

# PART IV

## The STEAM Power Challenge

.........................................................

# CHAPTER 16

# The STEAM Power Challenge

·······································

**I**t is valuable to learn how creativity can lead to innovations and connections, but let me offer this one final challenge to reinforce what we've been learning about: I invite you to learn a new STEAM skill. You can try working with a new technology you found interesting in this book; you can explore one of the skills that fall under any of the disciplines; you can even take a field trip to a local museum, makerspace, or learning center that incorporates STEAM and choose an unfamiliar area to explore.

I suggest you choose a technology, project, or area that is foreign to you because you'll end up learning more. Leaping into the unknown can make you anxious, but if you alter your mindset, that same energy can be seen as excitement. There is great freedom in taking on something you know nothing about because there is no expectation of you succeeding, and every moment involved leads to new learning. It can be a wonderful mess, but you will walk away with new knowledge that will likely aid you later.

We discussed how important connections and collaboration are in this process, so share your experience and your learning

Share your new STEAM skills, learning, ideas, and experiences with the projects from this book on Twitter using #ISTESteamPower. Let's build a stronger STEAM community!

on social media. I've created the hashtag #ISTESTEAMPower especially for this challenge, so I can help support you and your students as well.

Here are the basic steps:

1. Choose a STEAM project, technology, or area you're interested in exploring.

2. Let go of any expectations or previously conceived ideas you have about it that might be negative, nerve-racking, or put too much pressure on the experience.

3. Share out your choice on social media using the #ISTESTEAMPower hashtag.

4. Dive in and explore the topic. Document the process, including the successes and mistakes along the way. If you get stuck or frustrated, don't be afraid to ask for help!

5. Share the results, and even more importantly, the learning. It doesn't have to conclude in a massive success for you to have learned a great deal. If it's your first time trying to work with something new, just getting through the process is a success.

# STEAM POWER
# PROJECT RESOURCES

## Chapter 3: Classic Construction, Cardboard, and Upcycling

. . . . . . . . . . . . . . . . . . . . . . . . . . . . . . . . . . . . . . . . . . . . .

### Project: Upcycled Self-Watering Planter

**Wikipedia: Hydroponics**
An outline and definition of hydroponics and hydroculture
en.m.wikipedia.org/wiki/Hydroponics

**Pinterest: Upcycled Self-Watering Planter**
My Pinterest self-watering planter page
pinterest.com/mrtimneedles/upcycled-hydroponic-self-watering-planter

**NASA: Biofarming**
A historical NASA webpage covering hydroponics and biofarming
nasa.gov/missions/science/biofarming.html

**NASA: Deep-Space Food Crops**
An updated NASA webpage covering hydroponic potato crop studies
nasa.gov/feature/nasa-plant-researchers-explore-question-of-deep-space-food-crops

**Hydroponics Lesson Plan**
A hydroponics lesson plan with resources for supplies
settlement.arc.nasa.gov/teacher/lessons/contributed/thomas/hydroponics/hydroponics.html

## Project: Cardboard Chair Design

**Wikipedia: Cardboard Furniture**
Wikipedia page on cardboard furniture, featuring notable styles and techniques
en.wikipedia.org/wiki/Cardboard_furniture

**Pinterest: Cardboard Chair Design**
My Pinterest board on cardboard chairs
pinterest.com/mrtimneedles/cardboard-chair-design

**Museum of Modern Art: Frank Gehry Cardboard Chair Designs**
moma.org/artists/2108

**Cooper Hewitt Museum: Cardboard Design Collection**
tiny.cc/8ui6fz

# Chapter 4: Film, Video, and Animation

. . . . . . . . . . . . . . . . . . . . . . . . . . . . . . . . . . . . . . . . .

## Project: Video Poem

**PC Mag: Best Video Editing Software**
A list of video editing software with comparisons and data
pcmag.com/roundup/291335/the-best-video-editing-software

**Creative Bloq: The Best Video Editing Apps in 2020**
A list of video editing apps and their features
creativebloq.com/features/6-great-video-editing-apps-for-mobile

### General Poetry Resources:

**Poets.org**
The Academy of American Poets website, which has multiple educational resources and a
    poetry archive
poets.org

**National Poetry Month**
Annual celebration of poetry that occurs every April
poets.org/national-poetry-month

**The Library of Congress Poetry Archive**
A "poem a day" resource and information about the national poet laureates
loc.gov/poetry

### ReadWriteThink
An educator resource supported by the National Council of Teachers of English
readwritethink.org

### The Kennedy Center's Arts Edge
A resource for arts education, with lesson plans, videos, and examples
artsedge.kennedy-center.org/educators/lessons?q=poetry

### Think Written
A list of 101 poetry prompts to inspire writing
thinkwritten.com/poetry-prompts/

### 826 Video
Videos and resources from a national youth writing network that has regional locations
826national.org/category/video

### Video Poem Examples
My own examples of video poetry from my YouTube Page
youtu.be/N9dUIH0Kl-8

### The United States of Poetry
A PBS series of video poems from producer Joshua Blum and poet Bob Holman
bobholman.com/usop

### JWT-NY Video Poems featuring Billy Collins
A series of video poems
youtube.com/user/JWTNY/videos

## Project: Educational Public Service Announcement

### Storyboarding Blog Post
A blog post I created to help students understand how storyboarding works, with student examples
artroom161.blogspot.com/2019/02/digital-media-short-short-film-project.html

### *The Washington Post:* The 10 best PSAs of all time
tiny.cc/5t07fz

### TeachWriting.org: A How-To Guide for Teachers
A resource on how to write a PSA
teachwriting.org/blog/2018/4/11/public-service-announcements-a-how-to-guide-for -teachers

**Kathy Schrock's Guide to Everything**
A fellow Adobe Ed Leader's resource page for PSAs
schrockguide.net/psa.html

**Environmental Protection Agency: Public Service Announcements**
The EPA's collection of PSAs
epa.gov/newsroom/public-service-announcements

**My Video PSA Examples**
My video examples of student-produced PSAs
youtu.be/7DzrDi8Dfes

# Chapter 5: Digital Photography

. . . . . . . . . . . . . . . . . . . . . . . . . . . . . . . . . . . . . . . . . . . . . . .

## Project: Cyanotypes

**Wikipedia: Cyanotypes**
Wikipedia page on the history, process, and toning techniques of cyanotypes
en.wikipedia.org/wiki/Cyanotype

**Pinterest: Cyanotypes**
My Pinterest cyanotypes page
pinterest.com/mrtimneedles/cyanotypes

**The Science Company**
A resource for the use of cyanotype chemicals, including different recipes
sciencecompany.com/The-Cyanotype-Process.aspx

**Brooklyn Brainery**
A makerspace how-to for cyanotypes with images
brooklynbrainery.com/blog/try-this-cyanotype-prints

**The Phillips Collection**
A resource on the history of the cyanotype with instructions on caring for them
blog.phillipscollection.org/2012/05/04/what-is-a-cyanotype

**The Getty Museum**
A PDF publication, by Dusan C. Stulik and Art Kaplan, on the analytical signature of
    cyanotypes
getty.edu/conservation/publications_resources/pdf_publications/pdf/atlas_cyanotype.pdf

*The New York Times:* **Photography's Blue Period Is Making a Comeback**
An article on the resurgence of the cyanotype
nytimes.com/2016/02/06/arts/design/cyanotype-photographys-blue-period-is-making-a
  -comeback.html

**Make Magazine**
An article on photographer Meghann Riepenhoff's technique of using cyanotypes to
  create images from waves and sand
makezine.com/2016/01/15/radical-cyanotype-process-meghann-riepenhoff

## Project: Light Painting

**Wikipedia: Light Painting**
Wikipedia page on the history and various techniques of light painting
en.wikipedia.org/wiki/Light_painting

**Pinterest: Light Painting**
My Pinterest light painting page
pinterest.com/mrtimneedles/light-painting

**Light Painting Brushes**
An archive of tutorial videos, techniques, artists, tools, and contests
lightpaintingbrushes.com/pages/light-painting-tutorials

**Digital Photography School**
A resource for the terminology and basics of the light painting process
digital-photography-school.com/beginners-guide-to-light-painting

**Resource Magazine**
An archive of light paintings Gjon Mili created with Pablo Picasso for *Life Magazine*
resourcemagonline.com/2013/04/light-drawings-by-pablo-picasso-and-gjon-mili/24125

# Chapter 6: Web Design, Social Media, and Podcasting

. . . . . . . . . . . . . . . . . . . . . . . . . . . . . . . . . . . . .

## Project: STEAM Trading Cards

**ReadWriteThink**
A trading card creator tool, with lesson plans and examples
readwritethink.org/classroom-resources/student-interactives/trading-card-creator-30056.html

### WikiHow: Trading Cards

A wiki page with step-by-step instructions on how to create custom trading cards

wikihow.com/Make-Your-Own-Trading-Cards

### Wikipedia: Artist Trading Cards

Wikipedia page featuring the history and examples of artist trading cards

en.wikipedia.org/wiki/Artist_trading_cards

### Pinterest: Artist Trading Cards

My Pinterest page of artist trading cards, for inspiration on STEAM trading cards

pinterest.com/mrtimneedles/artist-trading-cards

### Quizlet

My list of STEAM influencers from history

quizlet.com/241239580/the-steam-power-historical-influencers-flash-cards/

### ARTROOM 161

My class blog, showing student and professional examples of artist and STEAM trading cards

artroom161.blogspot.com/search?q=atc

### Techwalla: How to Create a Trading Card in Photoshop

Step-by-step instructions for creating a trading card in Adobe Photoshop

techwalla.com/articles/how-to-create-a-trading-card-in-photoshop

## Project: STEAM Podcast Interview

### Wikipedia: Podcast

Wikipedia page featuring the history and well-known examples of podcasts

en.m.wikipedia.org/wiki/Podcast

### StoryCorps: Great Thanksgiving Listen

The Great Thanksgiving Listen page, with resources and instructions on using the
*StoryCorps* app

storycorps.org/participate/the-great-thanksgiving-listen

### StoryCorps: YouTube page

The most shared videos from *StoryCorps*. In class, I share "Q & A" and "No More
Questions!"

youtu.be/WNfvuJr9164

### NPR: Student Podcast Challenge

npr.org/2018/11/15/650500116/npr-student-podcast-challenge-home

### How to Start a Podcast
A resource with step-by-step instructions on how to create a podcast

thepodcasthost.com/planning/how-to-start-a-podcast

### Buffer
A guide to interviewing subjects, with tips from professionals

buffer.com/resources/6-powerful-communication-tricks-from-some-of-the-worlds-best
-interviewers

### Podcast Insights
An article on apps to use for recording and editing audio

podcastinsights.com/best-podcast-recording-software

# Chapter 7: Coding

. . . . . . . . . . . . . . . . . . . . . . . . . . . . . . . . . . . . . . . . . . .

## Project: Code Art

### Pinterest: Code Art
My Pinterest code art page for inspiration

pinterest.com/mrtimneedles/art-made-with-code

### Code.org: The Artist
A simple tutorial on how to create art with Blockly code

studio.code.org/s/artist/stage/1/puzzle/1

### Scratch
A gallery of art created using Scratch

scratch.mit.edu/studios/21720

### Code Fellows
An article describing art that can be created with code

codefellows.org/blog/creating-art-code

### Sean Justice
Contributor Sean Justice's examples of code art

seanjustice.com/codepoetry.html

### Rafael Lozano-Hemmer
Examples from an artist who uses code in interesting ways in many of his works

lozano-hemmer.com/projects.php

### Zach Lieberman
An artist who uses code, creates apps, and shares his process
zach.li

### HackerRank
An interview with Gerard Ferrandez on creating art with code
blog.hackerrank.com/creating-art-with-code

### YouTube: Creators
A Creators Project video with Casey Reas, showing how to draw with code
youtube.com/watch?v=_8DMEHxOLQE

### The Atlantic
A gallery of art created with code
theatlantic.com/technology/archive/2010/08/creating-art-with-code/61779

### Dev Art
A gallery of art created with code
devart.withgoogle.com

### MIT Alumni
Another example of creating art with code
alum.mit.edu/slice/creating-art-code

## Project: Video Games

### Wikipedia: Video Games
Wikipedia page on video games in education
en.wikipedia.org/wiki/Video_games_in_education

### Code Mom
A list of apps and programs to create video games for kids
codemom.ai/make-your-own-game-apps-for-kids

### Code.org
Short tutorials on creating video games for Hour of Code
code.org/hourofcode/overview

### WikiHow: Make Your Own Video Game
A step-by-step guide to creating a video game
wikihow.com/Make-Your-Own-Video-Game

### Scholastic Art and Writing Awards
An arts awards challenge for students with a video game section
artandwriting.org/what-we-do/the-awards/categories/#24

**Games for Change**
A video game challenge for students
gamesforchange.org

**Gamer Sensei**
An article on the benefits of video games in education
gamersensei.com/article/gaming-and-education

**High School Esports League**
A STEM.org approved Esports league for students
highschoolesportsleague.com

# Chapter 8: Digital Drawing and Design

## Project: Digital Self-Portrait

**Pinterest: Digital Portrait Drawings**
My Pinterest page on digital portrait drawing, for inspiration, techniques, and examples
pinterest.com/mrtimneedles/digital-portrait

**Creative Bloq: The Best Software for Digital Artists**
A resource reviewing software for digital drawing
creativebloq.com/advice/the-best-software-for-digital-artists

**Paintable**
Resources for digital drawing, including programs, tutorials, videos, and brushes
paintable.cc/resources

**YouTube: Paintable**
Tips and tricks for digital drawing and painting
youtube.com/watch?v=EuCykNjU0_w

**Ctrl+Paint**
A collection of free videos on digital drawing
ctrlpaint.com

**ARTROOM 161**
My class blog with examples of student self-portraits and the process of creating them
artroom161.blogspot.com/search/label/Digital%20Media%3A%20Digital%20Self%20
     Portrait%20Drawing

### Deviant Art

A collection of artwork, including a vast digital library of drawings (Before sending your students here, check that the content is appropriate for them.)

deviantart.com/deviations/visual-art/original-work/digital-art?page=1

## Project: STEAM Infographics

### Wikipedia: Infographics

Wikipedia page on the history of and tools for data visualization and infographics

en.wikipedia.org/wiki/Infographic

### Pinterest: Infographics

My Pinterest infographics page, for inspiration and examples

pinterest.com/mrtimneedles/infographics

### Creative Bloq

Fifty-six examples of great infographics

creativebloq.com/graphic-design-tips/information-graphics-1232836

### Visme

A collection of infographics in different subject areas

visme.co/blog/best-infographic-examples

### Creative Bloq

Nineteen infographic tools and programs

creativebloq.com/infographic/tools-2131971

### Canva

A free infographic creation tool

canva.com/create/infographics

### Design Dojo

Contributor Kevin McMahon's graphic design tutorials and resources for creating infographics

designdojo.org/projects

## Chapter 9: 3D Design, Printing, and Construction

. . . . . . . . . . . . . . . . . . . . . . . . . . . . . . . . . . . . . . . . . . .

## Project: 3D Architecture

### Wikipedia: 3D-Printed Architecture Construction

Wikipedia page on 3D-printed architecture, with history and examples

en.wikipedia.org/wiki/Construction_3D_printing

### Pinterest: 3D-Printed Architecture Design

My Pinterest 3D-printed architecture page, for inspiration and examples

pinterest.com/mrtimneedles/3d-printed-architecture

### SEArch+ (Space Exploration Architecture)

Information on the 3D-printed Mars Ice House, contributor Melodie Yashar's project with SEArch+ and winner of NASA's Centennial 3D-Printed Habitat on Mars Challenge

spacexarch.com/mars-ice-house

### Dezeen

An article on how 3D printing is changing architecture

dezeen.com/2013/05/21/3d-printing-architecture-print-shift

### i.materialize

An article with images about how printing 3D models can benefit architects

i.materialise.com/blog/en/3d-printing-for-architects

## Project: 3D Fashion Design

### Pinterest: 3D-Printed Fashion Design

My Pinterest 3D-printed fashion page, for inspiration and examples

pinterest.com/mrtimneedles/3d-printed-fashion

### 3D Natives

An article about designer Danit Peleg's customizable 3D-printed jacket

3dnatives.com/en/danit-peleg-3d-jacket020820174/

### Dezeen

An article on threeASFOUR 3D-printed dresses and runway show

dezeen.com/2016/02/17/3d-printed-dresses-threeasfour-new-york-fashion-week-2016

### CNET

An article on Anouk Wipprecht's robotic 3D-printed Spider Dress, with images and video

cnet.com/g00/news/robotic-spider-dress-defends-your-personal-space

### Names Dress

Sylvia Heisel's 3D-printed dress with the names of women in STEAM

namesdress.com/about

### All3DP

A resource outlining the current state of 3D-printed fashion, including examples

all3dp.com/2/3d-printed-fashion-the-state-of-the-art-in-2019

### 3DPrint.com
An article on designers who use 3D printing, with process and example images

3dprint.com/235318/revolutionary-fashion-designers-who-use-3d-printing-in-their-designs

### BluEdge
An article about twelve designers who have embraced 3D printing with images

bluedge.com/blog/miscellaneous/12-fashion-designers-whove-embraced-3d-printing

### 3D-Printed Art & Design World
An article about current 3D printing in fashion, with examples

3dprintedart.stratasys.com/new-blog/2018/7/16/discover-the-latest-in-3d-printing-for-fashion-design

# Chapter 10: Robotics and Drones

. . . . . . . . . . . . . . . . . . . . . . . . . . . . . . . . . . . . . . . . . . . .

## Project: Random Drawing Robot

### Design Boom: Drawing Machines
A collection of different professional and amateur drawing robots

designboom.com/tag/drawing-machines

### National Geographic
*National Geographic* videos and resources on robotics

nationalgeographic.org/education/robots-3d-education

### Makerspaces.com
A step-by-step guide to creating a bristlebot

makerspaces.com/how-to-make-a-bristlebot

### Make
A step-by-step guide to creating a brushbot

makezine.com/projects/building-brushbot-kits

### littleBits
A step-by-step guide to creating a drawing robot with littleBits

classroom.littlebits.com/lessons/drawing-bots-generative-art-machines

### Instructables: Arduino Drawing Robot
A step-by-step guide to creating a drawing robot with Arduino

instructables.com/id/Arduino-Drawing-Robot

**YouTube: Brainergiser**
A step-by-step guide to creating a spirograph robot drawing machine
youtube.com/watch?v=PBkwgaEli7w

**Pinterest: Robots in Education**
A Pinterest board of robots used in education for all grade levels and ages
pinterest.com/mrtimneedles/robots-in-education

## Project: Drone Photography

**Wikipedia: Unmanned Aerial Vehicle**
Wikipedia page on drones, including history, applications, markets, and regulations
en.wikipedia.org/wiki/Unmanned_aerial_vehicle

**Canva**
A beginner's guide to using drones for photography
canva.com/learn/the-complete-beginners-guide-to-drone-photography

**Bored Panda: Aerial Photography Contest 2018**
A collection of inspiring drone photographs
boredpanda.com/aerial-photography-contest-2018-dronestagram

**DroneZon**
A list of drones and drone kits for education
tiny.cc/hkx7fz

**Digital Camera World: Buying Guide**
A list of drones for photography
digitalcameraworld.com/buying-guides/the-10-best-camera-drones

**Drone Nodes: How to Build a Drone**
A resource for building your own drone, with comparisons and elements to consider
dronenodes.com/how-to-build-a-drone

# Chapter 11: Augmented and Virtual Reality

· · · · · · · · · · · · · · · · · · · · · · · · · · · · · · · · · · · · · · · · · · · ·

## Project: Augmented Reality Career Exploration

**Careers in STEM**
An alphabetical list of careers in STEM
careerinstem.com/stem-careers-list-alphabetical

**US News & World Reports**

A *US News & World Reports* list ranking the thirty best STEM careers, with data and
average salaries

money.usnews.com/careers/best-jobs/rankings/best-stem-jobs

**Digital Trends**

Examples of augmented reality apps

digitaltrends.com/mobile/best-augmented-reality-apps

**Drobots Company**

An educational drone competition for students, schools, clubs, and nonprofits

drobotscompany.com/drone-stem-competition-grades-1-12-high-school-kids-teens

## Project: Virtual Reality Drawing

**Pinterest: VR Drawing**

A collection of virtual reality drawings

pinterest.com/mrtimneedles/virtual-reality-drawing

**Digital Arts Online**

An article on programs and tools for virtual reality drawing

digitalartsonline.co.uk/features/hacking-maker/7-best-tools-for-painting-3d-modelling
-sculpting-in-vr

**Ideo**

A diary of a designer learning how to draw in VR, with images and video

ideo.com/blog/a-designers-daily-diary-of-learning-to-draw-in-vr

**Fast Company**

An article showing six artists and designers drawing in virtual reality

fastcompany.com/3059140/watch-six-artists-and-designers-draw-in-virtual-reality

**YouTube: SoulPancake's Art Attack**

A video showing a live drawn re-creation of Pablo Picasso's painting *Weeping Woman*

youtu.be/NLrOQcrNhXk

**Google Edu: Yale Case Study**

A case study of students learning to work with VR/AR at Yale University School of Arts

edu.google.com/why-google/case-studies/yale-vrar

# ISTE STANDARDS PROJECT MAPPING GUIDE

· · · · · · · · · · · · · · · · · · · · · · · · · · · · · · · · · · · ·

| PROJECT | ISTE Standards for Students |
|---|---|
| **Chapter 3:** Classic Construction: Upcycled Self-Watering Planter | **4. Innovative Designer** Students use a variety of technologies within a design process to identify and solve problems by creating new, useful or imaginative solutions. a. Students know and use a deliberate design process for generating ideas, testing theories, creating innovative artifacts or solving authentic problems. |
| **Chapter 3:** Classic Construction: Cardboard Chair Design | **4. Innovative Designer** Students use a variety of technologies within a design process to identify and solve problems by creating new, useful or imaginative solutions. c. Students develop, test and refine prototypes as part of a cyclical design process. |
| **Chapter 4:** Film, Video, and Animation: Video Poem | **6. Creative Communicator** Students communicate clearly and express themselves creatively for a variety of purposes using the platforms, tools, styles, formats and digital media appropriate to their goals. b. Students create original works or responsibly repurpose or remix digital resources into new creations. |
| **Chapter 4:** Film, Video, and Animation: Educational Public Service Announcement | **6. Creative Communicator** Students communicate clearly and express themselves creatively for a variety of purposes using the platforms, tools, styles, formats and digital media appropriate to their goals. d. Students publish or present content that customizes the message and medium for their intended audiences. |

| PROJECT | ISTE Standards for Students |
|---|---|
| Chapter 5: Digital Photography: Cyanotype | **6. Creative Communicator**<br>Students communicate clearly and express themselves creatively for a variety of purposes using the platforms, tools, styles, formats and digital media appropriate to their goals.<br>b. Students create original works or responsibly repurpose or remix digital resources into new creations. |
| Chapter 5: Digital Photography: Light Painting | **7. Global Collaborator**<br>Students use digital tools to broaden their perspectives and enrich their learning by collaborating with others and working effectively in teams locally and globally.<br>c. Students contribute constructively to project teams, assuming various roles and responsibilities to work effectively toward a common goal. |
| Chapter 6: Web Design, Social Media, and Podcasting: STEAM Trading Cards | **3. Knowledge Constructor**<br>Students critically curate a variety of resources using digital tools to construct knowledge, produce creative artifacts and make meaningful learning experiences for themselves and others.<br>c. Students curate information from digital resources using a variety of tools and methods to create collections of artifacts that demonstrate meaningful connections or conclusions. |
| Chapter 6: Web Design, Social Media, and Podcasting: STEAM Podcast Interview | **2. Digital Citizen**<br>Students recognize the rights, responsibilities and opportunities of living, learning and working in an interconnected digital world, and they act and model in ways that are safe, legal and ethical.<br>a. Students cultivate and manage their digital identity and reputation and are aware of the permanence of their actions in the digital world. |
| Chapter 7: Coding: Code Art | **5. Computational Thinker**<br>Students develop and employ strategies for understanding and solving problems in ways that leverage the power of technological methods to develop and test solutions.<br>d. Students understand how automation works and use algorithmic thinking to develop a sequence of steps to create and test automated solutions. |
| Chapter 7: Coding: Video Games | **5. Computational Thinker**<br>Students develop and employ strategies for understanding and solving problems in ways that leverage the power of technological methods to develop and test solutions.<br>c. Students break problems into component parts, extract key information, and develop descriptive models to understand complex systems or facilitate problem-solving. |
| Chapter 8: Digital Drawing and Design: Digital Self-Portrait | **6. Creative Communicator**<br>Students communicate clearly and express themselves creatively for a variety of purposes using the platforms, tools, styles, formats and digital media appropriate to their goals.<br>a. Students choose the appropriate platforms and tools for meeting the desired objectives of their creation or communication. |

| PROJECT | ISTE Standards for Students |
|---|---|
| **Chapter 8:** Digital Drawing and Design: STEAM Infographics | **6. Creative Communicator** Students communicate clearly and express themselves creatively for a variety of purposes using the platforms, tools, styles, formats and digital media appropriate to their goals. c. Students communicate complex ideas clearly and effectively by creating or using a variety of digital objects such as visualizations, models or simulations. |
| **Chapter 9:** Design, Printing, and Construction: 3D Architecture | **7. Global Collaborator** Students use digital tools to broaden their perspectives and enrich their learning by collaborating with others and working effectively in teams locally and globally. d. Students explore local and global issues and use collaborative technologies to work with others to investigate solutions. |
| **Chapter 9:** Design, Printing, and Construction: 3D Fashion Design | **4. Innovative Designer** Students use a variety of technologies within a design process to identify and solve problems by creating new, useful or imaginative solutions. b. Students select and use digital tools to plan and manage a design process that considers design constraints and calculated risks. |
| **Chapter 10:** Robotics and Drones: Random Drawing Robot | **4. Innovative Designer** Students use a variety of technologies within a design process to identify and solve problems by creating new, useful or imaginative solutions. d. Students exhibit a tolerance for ambiguity, perseverance and the capacity to work with open-ended problems. |
| **Chapter 10:** Robotics and Drones: Drone Photography | **2. Digital Citizen** Students recognize the rights, responsibilities and opportunities of living, learning and working in an interconnected digital world, and they act and model in ways that are safe, legal and ethical. b. Students engage in positive, safe, legal and ethical behavior when using technology, including social interactions online or when using networked devices. |
| **Chapter 11:** Augmented and Virtual Reality: Augmented Reality Career Exploration | **1. Empowered Learner** Students leverage technology to take an active role in choosing, achieving and demonstrating competency in their learning goals, informed by the learning sciences. a. Students articulate and set personal learning goals, develop strategies leveraging technology to achieve them and reflect on the learning process itself to improve learning outcomes. |
| **Chapter 11:** Augmented and Virtual Reality: Virtual Reality Drawing | **1. Empowered Learner** Students leverage technology to take an active role in choosing, achieving and demonstrating competency in their learning goals, informed by the learning sciences. d. Students understand the fundamental concepts of technology operations, demonstrate the ability to choose, use and troubleshoot current technologies and are able to transfer their knowledge to explore emerging technologies. |

# REFERENCES

. . . . . . . . . . . . . . . . . . . . . . . . . .

Dalí, S. (1993). *The secret life of Salvador Dalí.* New York, NY: Dover Publications.

Dweck, C. (2016). *Mindset: The new psychology of success.* New York, NY: Ballantine.

Einstein, A. (October, 1929). What life means to Einstein: An interview by George Sylvester Viereck. *The Saturday Evening Post.*

Hubbard, E. (1908). *Little journeys to the homes of great teachers.* East Aurora, NY: The Roycrofters.

Jacob, B. A. (2004). To catch a cheat. *Education Next, 4*(1).

Myers, D. (2001). Why blame the tests for exposing unequal experiences and opportunities? *Psychology.* New York, NY: Worth Publishers.

Pink, D. H. (2009). *Drive: The surprising truth about what motivates us.* New York, NY: Riverhead Books.

Zuriff, G.E. (1997). Accommodations for test anxiety under ADA? *Journal of the American Academy of Psychiatry and the Law, 25*(2), 198-206.

# INDEX

. . . . . . . . . . . . . .

# Your opinion matters:
# Tell us how we're doing!

Your feedback helps ISTE create the best possible resources for teaching and learning in the digital age. Share your thoughts with the community or tell us how we're doing!

You can:

- Write a review at amazon.com or barnesandnoble.com.
- Join conversations about the book using the hashtag #ISTESTEAMPower
- Mention this book on social media and follow ISTE on Twitter @iste, Facebook @ISTEconnects or Instagram @isteconnects
- Email us at books@iste.org with your questions or comments.